YO-EMJ-269

Reptiles as Pets

REPTILES AS PETS

PAUL VILLIARD

With Photographs by the Author

Doubleday & Company, Inc., Garden City, New York

FOR DEAN . . .

AN EARNEST FRIEND OF REPTILES

Acknowledgments

I should like to extend my thanks to the many persons who helped me put this book together. To Mr. Paul W. Beard, of Monterey, California, and Mr. Jim Westra of *Animal Kingdom* in Grand Rapids, Michigan—both of whom sent much material for photographs and habit study.

To Dean Davis for the freely offered help in managing my specimens and loaning his own for photographing.

To my sons, William and Paul, who energetically gleaned the fields for specimens.

And, of course, to Gertrude, my wife, who spent most of her waking hours tending all the animals throughout the house, cleaning their cages, feeding them and caring for them during the course of building this book, goes my special thanks.

Contents

Contents

Preface

Whenever anybody says "reptile" he usually is thinking of a snake. Many people, whenever they think of snakes, are afraid. People have been afraid of snakes for thousands of years. Sometimes it seems that the only people who do not fear them are small boys—and even some of them dislike snakes.

This is really too bad. Snakes are not evil. In fact, they are among the most useful and valuable animals living today. And they are very interesting!

When we speak of the natural food of animals, we mean food that those kinds of animals like best to eat. The natural food of many snakes is rats, mice, and other destructive rodents.

Farmers used to chop up every snake they saw with a hoe just because it was a snake. Out of fear, they would say, "There's a snake, kill it!" In the past few years, much has been learned about snakes and other reptiles. Now farmers are not in such a hurry to kill the animals that may help keep their barns free of pests.

Many farmers now like to see a snake in the barn. Some of them have even bought snakes and let them loose on their farms in order to help keep the rats and mice under control. The best snakes for this work are bull snakes, corn snakes, rat snakes, chicken snakes, king snakes, and milk snakes. King snakes and milk snakes are different members of the same group. Rat snakes, corn snakes, and chicken snakes are all members of another group. The bull snake belongs to yet another group. All of these animals should be left alone when they are found, because each year every specimen will eat a very great number of rats and mice.

Some snakes are poisonous and can kill people by biting them. Obviously, poisonous snakes should not be kept as pets, except in a zoo or by experienced *herpetologists*. A herpetologist is a person who studies reptiles. The name comes from *herpes*, which is a Greek word meaning "to creep," even though not all reptiles creep.

Snakes are not the only reptiles. Turtles, lizards, geckos, and skinks are also reptiles. Geckos, lizards, and skinks look very much alike, but they belong to different groups. Frogs and toads are not reptiles. They are *amphibians.* Amphibians are animals which must return to water in order to breed and lay their eggs.

Not very many lizards are poisonous. There is only one species in the United States and one in Mexico. Turtles and geckos are not poisonous, and neither are skinks.

Turtles, skinks, geckos, and lizards can bite. Some of them bite hard, and will tear your skin. Some non-poisonous snakes can bite, too, and some of the large ones can hurt. The bites are not dangerous unless they become infected. Any time you are bitten by a reptile, you should dab some disinfectant on the bite and cover it with a bandage to keep it clean.

Most animals bite only from fear and in self-protection. If they are handled gently, as if they have nothing to be afraid of, they will stop trying to bite every time you pick them up.

Nearly all animals will try to bite if they are ready to have their young, or already have had them. But snakes and other reptiles are different. They do not protect their young or eggs. They might even eat them if the babies cannot escape fast enough! Reptiles do not have any *maternal instinct*, which means that they do not take care of their young. They lay their eggs in a sand pile, or under a log, and leave them

"Glass Snake" guarding her eggs. The guarding consists of curling around them for a time. If she remains with the eggs, the chances are she will eat them!

13

alone to hatch. A few snakes and lizards curl up around their eggs, but they are not protecting them. If the animal is disturbed, it will leave the eggs.

If you want to keep reptiles as pets, you should learn as much about their behavior as you can. There are many books that tell you things about reptiles. Although many of these books are very difficult to understand, because they are research textbooks and were written for reference libraries, there are several books, including this one, written just to tell young people about the lives and habits of reptiles, and these should be read as carefully as possible. The more you learn about the animals, the better chance you have of being able to keep them healthy and contented.

Unless you know about an animal, you should never try to keep it as a pet. If you find an unusual reptile in the pet shop and the clerk does not know the real name of it, or what it eats, or how warm it should be kept, it would be better to leave it there and not try to take it home. Without proper care it will die very soon. Many thousands of reptiles die every year because the people who sell them and the people who buy them do not know how to keep them. In this book I am going to try to tell you about many different kinds of reptiles and how to keep them at home. Different reptiles need different conditions to remain healthy. Some need warmth. Others must be kept really hot. Still others will die unless they are kept cool. Some of them cannot drink water from a dish. These kinds of reptiles die very quickly after they are brought home.

Some reptiles are *nocturnal.* This means that they are active only at night, which is the only time you will really see how they go about their lives. Other reptiles are *diurnal,* or active in the daytime. Still a third group are *crepuscular.* This group is active in the early light of dawn and the dim light of evening. Many desert reptiles are crepuscular. This way they avoid the great heat of the daytime and the cold of the night.

Knowing about all these things makes it easier to take care of the little animals.

Many reptiles are *solitary*. They like to be alone, and cannot be kept in a cage with other reptiles. They will either fight their companion or huddle in a corner. Usually, two males cannot be kept together, because they will fight. Large specimens should never be kept with small specimens. The big ones will often eat the little ones—even if they are the same kind, and even if the small ones are offspring of the big ones!

If you know these things when you get your pet turtle, snake, or lizard, you will stand a better chance of keeping it as a pet. If you do not know things about the animals, then you do not have pets, just captive reptiles. They will suffer for a while and then die. Reptiles cannot tell you when they are suffering. There isn't any way you can tell, either, until suddenly they die. The trouble is that they do not die suddenly, but suffer for a long, long time first.

There are many legends about reptiles. These stories are mostly about snakes, and most of the stories are not true. There is a story about the big rattlesnake that killed a man by biting him in the foot—right through his heavy boot. Then, years after the man had died, his son put on the boots and was killed by the fang of the rattlesnake, which had broken off and was still sticking through the boot!

Another untrue story is about mud snakes, which, in the South, are called hoop snakes. This story is that the hoop snake will take its tail in its mouth, roll like a hoop, chasing a person down the road, and, when it catches the person, lash him with its tail and poison him. The snake cannot roll like a hoop, and it is not poisonous.

Some of the people in the South say the hog-nosed snake

is the most venomous snake in the country. There is a story that the breath of this snake can kill a man at a distance of from twenty-five to thirty feet! This poor, helpless animal usually feeds on toads and rarely tries to bite a person, even when it is captured. It spreads its neck out flat and hisses loudly to frighten off its attacker, and will even play dead, trying to escape. It is one of the most harmless snakes in the world, and makes a wonderful pet.

The story about the "glass snake" that will break into a dozen pieces, and then, after being left alone, will join together again, is also not true. This animal is not even a snake; it is a legless lizard. It is true that the tail will break off if the lizard is roughly handled. But this is a way of protecting itself. If another animal tries to eat a "glass snake" and the tail drops off, the bit of tail will jump about and that is what the enemy will be watching while the rest of the lizard quietly sneaks off into the weeds to safety. A new tail will grow in, but not so long or so slender as the old one.

Stories about snakes a hundred feet long that eat everybody they come across are often told. Snakes do not grow that big. The largest snake on record is the anaconda from South America, which grows to about thirty-seven feet long. The great pythons of India reach thirty-three feet or more. Lizards do not grow so large. Iguanas can be six feet or more, and some of the monitors are nearly as large.

Reptiles as Pets

CHAPTER 1

A Little About Reptiles

In the beginning, animal life on earth was probably *proto-zoan*. Protozoan is a name made up of two Greek combining words: proto- meaning "first" and -zoa meaning "animal." After millions of years of evolution, larger animals developed, still living in the seas and warm fresh waters. Many of these animals laid eggs, but the eggs were soft and jelly-like and had to remain under water all the time to keep from drying out.

The animals themselves could leave the water for short periods to find food or to walk about on land. They had to stay near the water, though, because if their skins dried out, they would die. They had to go back into the water in order to breed and lay their eggs. These animals were called *amphibians,* and there are still some amphibians living today. Toads and frogs are amphibians. So are salamanders.

All amphibians have two things in common. All must return to the water to lay their eggs, and the young sometimes do not look like the adults, but go through a larval stage in the water. After a time, they undergo a very big change in habit and shape. This change is called *metamorphosis* and means "a change of shape." After metamorphosis, the amphibians then leave the water and live on land.

Frogs are good examples of amphibians. Everyone knows

about tadpoles swarming in brooks and ponds in the early summer. These are the larval stage of frogs and toads. The tadpoles change into frogs, which hop out of the water to live on the banks, eating insects and small creatures. They are always ready to hop back into the water when danger comes near.

Reptiles are different from amphibians in their breeding habits. Reptiles can either have their young alive, or they can lay eggs. If they give birth to live young, they are called *viviparous* reptiles. If they are the egg-laying kind, they are *oviparous* reptiles. The shells of reptile eggs are tough and rubbery. They are not brittle like a hen's egg, but soft and flexible.

If reptiles had not developed this kind of egg, there would not be any people on earth today. It was the ability to lay eggs that did not dry out that first made it possible for the reptiles to come out of the sea, and for life to start developing on the land parts of the world. Even so, the eggs of reptiles will dry out if they are not kept a little bit moist. If reptile eggs are kept in water, the moisture will go right through the shell and the *embryo* developing inside will drown. But they must not be exposed to the dry air for long periods of time, either.

No snake has real legs any more. Millions of years ago some snakes did have legs, but they gradually became useless. Some of the boas have two little stubs sticking out of the rear part of their bodies, but that is all that is left of their legs.

Snakes travel in several different ways. The usual way a snake gets around is by *undulating* its body. This means looping its long body from side to side, pushing against small stones, twigs, clumps of grass, and other things on the ground. As long as there is anything to push against, the snake can let its body flow around the stone or twig until it reaches another point to push against. It does this so rapidly that the snake doesn't seem to touch anything but just pours along the ground.

Another way the snake can move is by using the scales (called *scutes*) on its belly. Inside the snake's skin its ribs are attached to the ends of the scutes. A snake can move its ribs independently. Starting at the head, it can raise a pair of ribs and the scute attached to it, then push back against the ground with the scute. Each scute and pair of ribs follows the first one in a ripple down the body of the snake. The animal can move quite rapidly along the uneven ground by this method, but it usually undulates at the same time to gain speed—especially if it is running away from an enemy.

It is easier to tell the snake's body from its tail than you might think. On the belly side of every snake is an opening. This is sometimes called the vent. Its real name is a *cloaca* which is a Latin word meaning "sewer." A snake uses this opening for several purposes. It gets rid of its body wastes, lays its eggs, and mates through the cloaca. The same opening serves all these functions for the animal. A snake's body stops at the cloaca. Beyond this point is the tail. A large scale usually covers the vent, and in some snakes this scale is divided into two halves instead of being one large plate. The type of scale covering the vent (together with other markings) is used to identify different species of snakes. This scale is often referred to as an anal plate.

The scales on snakes' bodies differ, too. Some of them are very smooth and shiny. Others have a ridge running across them. It is said that these scales are *keeled*, because the ridges look like the keel on a boat. Water snakes generally have keeled scales. King snakes generally have smooth scales.

Snakes that live in places full of brush and twigs are often striped down the back. This helps them to hide among the sticks and shadows of twigs. Those that live on forest floors where there are fallen leaves and decaying underbrush often have spots or blotches down their backs. If this kind of snake stays still on a pile of leaves, it is almost impossible to see. The spots and blotches look like spots of sunlight on a dark pile of leaves.

Hybrid Pine Snake. *Pituophis melanoleucus*. The blotches on the skin of this snake tells you that it lives in the sun-speckled forest rather than in the grass.

Snakes that live in burrows and underground generally have skins that are plain color without any markings at all. They do not need anything to help them hide from their enemies.

Coral snakes are exceptions to this rule. They are very brightly colored. In fact, they are gaudy and stand out very clearly from their surroundings. This, too, is a way of protecting them from their enemies. Their brightly colored skins tell their enemies that they are dangerous, and that it is better to leave them alone. Coral snakes are very poisonous and their bite can be fatal. Some harmless snakes are colored like the coral snakes. This helps the harmless snakes escape their enemies because the enemies think they are looking at a dangerous snake instead of one that is good to eat.

The blotches and markings on animals' skins are called *protective coloration,* because they help the animals to hide. Copying the color or markings of one animal by another in order to protect itself from its enemies is called *mimicry.* The coral snake is a good example of the use of protective coloration and the harmless snakes that are colored almost like the coral snake are excellent examples of protective mimicry.

Since a snake has no eyelids, it cannot close its eyes at all. A snake's eyes are covered with a clear scale to protect them. The tongue of a snake is forked or double at the tip. It is kept in a tube in the bottom of the mouth. Generally there is a small opening at the lower front part of the jaw so the snake can stick out its tongue without opening its mouth.

Very often, as it crawls along, the snake sticks its tongue out and waves it up and down, then pulls it back into its mouth. In the tube that holds the tongue are special parts called Jacobson's organs. The tongue rubs across these organs when it is pulled into the mouth. Particles of air stick to the tongue when the animal moves it up and down. In this way, the snake can sense its food or enemies. It is not really either tasting or smelling, but scientists think it is a little bit of both. This is a special sense that we do not have. The tongue of a snake is perfectly harmless. No snake can hurt anything at all with it. And the snake is deaf, as it has no eardrums.

As snakes and other reptiles feed and grow larger, their skins become too small for their bodies, so they have to shed them. Most of the time a snake sheds its skin in one piece. Even the skin over the eyes is shed. For a day or two before shedding the snake is almost blind, because the old skin loosens over the eyes and becomes milky in color. During this time even very tame snakes are very much afraid, since they are almost helpless. At this time you should leave them alone as much as possible.

Head of Garter Snake. *Thamnophis sirtalis.* Just before shedding its skin, the snakes are almost blind. At this time they are easily frightened and are very nervous.

After the entire old skin is loose, the snake will catch its lips on a pebble or bark or other rough anchor. It will pull its lips and head out of the skin, then crawl right out of the entire skin—turning the old skin inside out as it goes. After shedding, the snake is very bright with colors that stand out. Some of the highly colored ones can be very beautiful then. The number of times a snake sheds its skin in a year depends on the amount of food it is able to eat, and on how fast it grows.

A snake can eat food many times larger than itself. The jaws of a snake come apart at the joints. The upper jaws can snap apart from the lower jaws, and the right sides separate from the left sides. The only thing holding the jaws together then is the skin, which can stretch like rubber.

The teeth of most snakes that have them curve backward in the jaw. When food is caught, these curved teeth can hold it firmly while the snake eats. Many snakes eat their food alive. They grasp hold of the prey and start to "walk" their jaws back and forth, gripping the prey with their curved teeth each time they push their jaws forward. The food slides easily down the throat of the snake, and it almost looks as though the prey crawls down by itself! Snakes that eat things like frogs, fish, toads, and insects usually have short teeth, while the teeth of snakes that eat rats, mice, and other furred or feathered animals are usually much longer. This is because the teeth of these snakes must reach through the fur or feathers in order to hold the prey while it is being eaten.

Snakes like the king snake, the rat snake, and pythons are called *constrictors*. This kind of snake catches its prey in its mouth, holding it with its teeth while it wraps its body around the prey and squeezes it until it is dead. Then it loosens its body and eats the prey.

It is not true that a constrictor cracks the bones of its prey and kneads the animal until it is soft before eating it. What the snake does is hold the animal so tightly that it cannot breathe. Each time the animal tries to take a breath the snake tightens its hold a little bit more, until finally the prey is smothered. When a constrictor catches an animal the action is so fast that you can hardly see what happens. One minute a mouse or rat will be near the snake and the next instant the snake will be wrapped around the prey—squeezing it to death. Most of the time the rat or mouse hasn't even time to squeak!

Lizards are very different from snakes. They usually have eyelids and can close their eyes. Many of them have a clear spot in the middle of the eyelid and can see through this spot with the lids shut. The eyelids of lizards close from the bottom up instead of from the top down the way human eyes do. Most lizards have legs, some of them very long, and they can be very fast runners. Some of the desert lizards can stand up and run on their hind legs, looking like small dinosaurs. One kind—the basilisk—can run so fast on its hind legs that it can actually run over the top of water for a short distance without sinking! Of course, if it slows down or stops, it sinks right away, but it can swim well, so this does not seem to bother it at all.

When a lizard sheds its skin, it usually comes off in patches instead of in one piece, like a snake's. A lizard almost always eats its skin after shedding. This is a protective device. If the lizard leaves its skin lying around where it was shed, enemies can see that it lives nearby and can hunt it down.

Lizards have ears and most of them can hear very well. The ears are inside and do not stick out on the head as ours do. There is an opening behind each eye that leads into the ear. In some lizards the opening is covered with a thin clear skin called a *tympanum*. The name is taken from a Latin word meaning "drum." A human eardrum is also called a tympanum. Some of the ear openings of lizards do not have this skin covering them, but have deep holes since the eardrum is inside the head. Some lizards have neither holes nor clear skin. These are called earless lizards. A few species of earless lizards live in the southwestern part of the United States.

Lizards usually have very sharp claws, which help them climb. Some of them live in trees most of the time, coming down to the ground only to lay their eggs. They can climb walls and curtains so fast that it is very hard to catch them if they get away from you. Many lizards live near water and go into it very often. The big iguanas of Central America and South America live in the trees on the riverbanks. When danger approaches they drop into the water. This makes it even harder to catch them.

Many lizards have the ability to drop their tails when attacked by an enemy. Their tails are divided into sections so they will snap off without much pain or bleeding. When an enemy pounces on the lizard, more often than not it is left with a wiggling part of tail while the body of the lizard scampers away. The tail jumps around for a long time after breaking off of the lizard. This is to keep the enemy occupied long enough for the lizard to make its escape. Animals that drop their tails like this can grow new tails, but usually the new ones are not so long or so pretty as the old ones, Sometimes the new tails grow in crooked or forked, or even double or triple. Lizards with two or three tails have been seen.

At least three species of lizard have no legs at all. These are the ones that are called "glass snakes" in the southern part of this country where they live. Usually glass snakes do not make good pets because they frighten too easily and are hard to feed. Whenever you see a smooth, shiny snake flowing through the grass and weeds, look closely at it if you can. If it has eyelids and can close its eyes, and has ear openings on each side of its head, then it is a legless lizard and not a snake at all. The bodies of these animals are rounder than a snake's body, and much firmer. There are usually stripes running down the sides and back.

A skink is a kind of lizard that is very timid and usually is active only at night. It stays under fallen logs and stones, and among the dry leaves in the forests. The skink is usually smooth and shiny-looking and very fast. It also drops its tail easily and bites when it is caught, but cannot do much damage. Some of the skinks are very brightly colored and are among the most beautiful of the lizards. They almost all have eyelids. When skinks run about they wiggle their bodies like snakes. The skinks (and some geckos) seem to wiggle more than other lizards. Skinks generally have more pointed heads and jaws than other lizards. And several kinds of skinks grow to be almost two feet long. These giants are not found in this country, but come from Australia.

Geckos are lizards with some interesting habits. They can walk almost any place and anywhere. Many of this group have toes covered with very tiny stiff hairs. The toes are flexible and bend both backward and forward. Geckos do not have suction pads on their feet as many people think. When a gecko runs or walks he puts his feet down with the toes curled backward, then flattens them out so the hairs grip the surface he is walking on. When he lifts his feet he first must curl his toes up to release the hairs. These animals can walk right up a windowpane by gripping the uneven surface of the glass with the hairs on their toes! They can run across a ceiling just as easily as across the floor.

Some geckos have eyelids and others do not. Geckos have a

Gecko's foot. The underside of a foot of the tokay gecko is made of many ridges, each one of which is made of hundreds of tiny stiff hooks. This enables the animal to run up a wall or over a ceiling.

Tokay Gecko. *Gekko gecko*. The pupils of the eyes of tokay geckos are wavy, and close to make four pinhole irises.

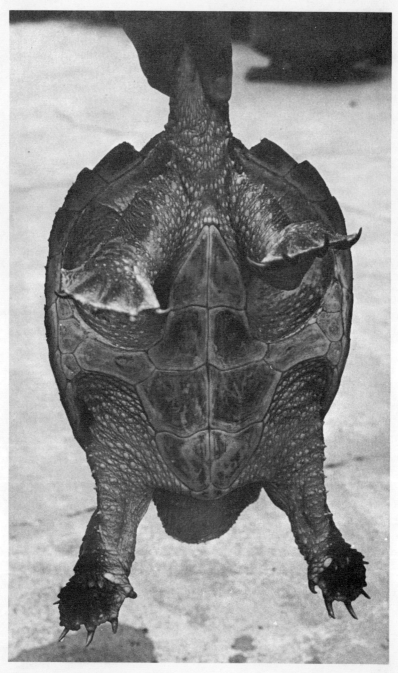

Snapping Turtle. *Chelydra serpentina*. Young specimens can be picked up by the tail, but this may kill them when they are older.

Snapping Turtle. *Chelydra serpentina.* If you do pick up a snapper by its tail, be sure to hold it away from you or it may take a good bite out of your leg!

funny way of cleaning their eyeballs. They do this by licking them with their tongue! Most geckos are night animals
with vertical pupils in their eyes; but some of them are
active both during the day and at night. The eyes of these
kinds of geckos have a special kind of iris. The pupil is
vertical, but instead of being straight like that of the night
gecko, it is wavy. When the gecko is in the bright light of
day, and the iris is tightly closed, three or four little pinholes
are left open by the wavy line, so the animal can see very
well without being blinded by the light. Many geckos have
very beautiful eyes. They are silver, gold, or brightly colored.
Sometimes they are two colors.

A very strange habit that geckos have is to pull their eyeballs back into their heads. This is frightening when you
first see it. You think that the animal is dying, or at least suffering. Tokay geckos are among the worst ones for this
trick. They do it when they feed and when they try to bite,
which is nearly every time you go near them.

Unlike many lizards and snakes, which can only hiss, the
gecko has a voice. It is not a true voice; the noise is made
by pulling air into or blowing it out of the lungs. Some
geckos can cheep or squeak, and the tokay gecko barks like
a small dog. When geckos are well fed, warm enough, and
contented, they will cheep throughout the night.

There are a great many different kinds of turtles. Not all
of them are good as pets, but most of them live for a long
time. Turtles are among the longest-lived animals on earth.

They are divided into groups. There are some turtles that
live on land all the time and do not need water. There are
others that must live in the water all the time. Then there
are turtles that live on land but need water to swim in. Some
of them will not feed unless they eat under water. Of course,
the turtles that live on land are the easiest kinds to keep.

Some of the water turtles are very interesting. The very ugly water turtle from South America called matamata is sold in pet stores. It does not bite. Its main food is fish and small *crustaceans.* Crustaceans are strange animals that wear their skeletons on the outsides of their bodies the way insects do. Lobsters and shrimps are crustaceans. So are crawfish, which you can see hiding in the mud in the bottoms of clear streams and meadow brooks.

Some turtles eat vegetables and fruit as well as meat, but others need meat all the time. Some turtles can give the worst bite of all reptiles. A big snapping turtle can take a real chunk out of your leg if you are not careful. Turtles like this do not make good pets. If you want to pick up a snapping turtle, use its long tail for a handle if the animal is not too big. Be careful that you hold the dangling reptile away from you, though, or you will lose part of your leg. It can bite upside down as well as right side up.

In the last few years scientists have discovered that some turtles carry a disease called *salmonella* and can give it to people. Unless you can be very clean around your turtle pets and keep them clean, too, it might be best if you did not have these animals as pets at all. If you can remember to wash your hands very well every time you handle your turtle, and not to keep the turtle in containers that might come in contact with you or with other members of your family, then a turtle could make a good pet. It will live a long time, eat readily, and should become tame very quickly.

CHAPTER 2

A Lesson in Taxonomy

Taxonomy is the science of classifying things. It is one of the most important parts of studying animals, plants, and minerals. There are people called *taxonomists* who make their living studying organisms and their names to make sure they are grouped correctly. As more information is discovered about a certain thing, the taxonomist often will find it belongs to a different group than it was in, and put it in the new group, with a new name.

Because there are so many different languages in the world, taxonomists had to find a language everyone could use. They chose Latin. The reason for this is that Latin is a "dead" language. This means that although Latin was once used as a means of verbal and written communication, it is not used any more. Unless a language is used all the time, it stops growing, new words are never added, and the language is called dead. A dead language is the best kind to use for naming things, because if the language is living the way English is, new words would always be added and new names made up so the scientists would have a very hard time keeping track of a name.

Thousands of years ago people did not even have good names for themselves. It took a long time and much talking for a person to tell another person who or what he was thinking about. Finally people started to give names to each other, and their children were always called "the son of." If you wanted to talk about a friend, you might say, "I saw George, the miller, today." After many hundreds of years, people started taking the names of what they did as their own names. This was called *occupational identification.* The man who ground up wheat for flour was known as Mr. Miller. The man who caught fish for the village came to be called Mr. Fisher. Still later, their children added "son" to their father's names so people would know who they were. The son of John became Mr. Johnson. Or the son of Jack, Mr. Jackson.

This kind of naming was all right for people, but it was not very good for plants or animals. Sometimes in writing a book a whole paragraph was used to describe just one animal so people would know which one it was. Finally a Swedish scientist named Carl von Linné had an idea. He took Latin, the dead language, and Greek, a living language. From the Greek he named the plants and animals in groups. This was like the name "Miller" for people. From the Latin he named each plant or animal for itself, like George. Scientists all over the world began to use Latin and Greek when they named anything, and every scientist could then know what other scientists were talking about. Linné even went so far as to name himself the same way that he named the animals, and his new name was Carolus Linnaeus, which is Latin for Carl von Linné. This way of naming things was called the *binomial* (two-names) *system* and it is used all over the world today.

It is very important to know the real names of animals or other things you are studying. If you only know the popular name it can be very confusing, and most of the time people will not know what you are talking about. Do you know what a scorpion is? You think it is some kind of "bug" that has a tail with a stinger on the end? Maybe it is, where you come from. But in the southern part of the United States, people call the blue-tailed skink a scorpion. The real scorpion is called a *vinegarroon*. The skink is a lizard, and not a "bug" at all, so you can see how important it is to know exactly what your animal is called.

Maybe you think that it makes no difference whether or not you know the name of the animal, since you are only keeping it for a pet. That could be true, if you were familiar with all the different animals you see. But suppose you got one in a pet shop that came from some other country clear across the world from you. If you could not tell the name of this animal, you might not be able to find out what it ate, whether it liked to be kept warm or cool, whether it needed water or a dry cage, or many other things important to keeping it alive.

You could hardly go up to some zoo or even a pet shop man and say, "I have an animal with green on its tail. It is about this long, it has four legs, and the body is green and blue with a white band on the neck. What does it eat?" The chances are the man could not tell you anything at all about your pet. But if you went to him and said, "I have a *Crotaphytus collaris*," any person who knew about reptiles could tell you a lot about it. Even if you only knew the popular name you could get information in a pet shop if you asked the man to tell you about your *collared lizard*. The Latin names are not at all hard to remember and to say. You will find that they break up into syllables and are very easy to read or say. For Crotaphytus, say, crot-a-fí-tus.

So, you see, you should learn both names of all the animals you try to keep as pets. The popular name will do very nicely when you are buying or collecting them, and when you want to get information from the pet store man. When you talk to a teacher or scientist about your pets, then you can use the real scientific name and *he* will know what you are talking about. Even if you go on a trip to another country and cannot speak the language, if you said *"Crotaphytus collaris"* to a scientist in Japan or in India or in any country in the world, he would smile and nod his head. He would know the animal you had.

All through this book I use the popular names for animals that are common in most parts of the United States. In the back of the book there is an index of their scientific names. You can learn both names and you should have no trouble getting to know your animals. You will be a junior taxonomist.

CHAPTER 3

How to Collect Reptiles and Where to Buy Them

Many reptiles that make good pets can be found in the woods and fields near where you live. If you live in big cities like New York or Chicago or San Francisco, then you have to go outside the city to find animals. A streetcar or a bus can take you to the edge of the city and you can look in the fields and woods nearby for your specimens.

If you go to camp during school vacation you have a very good chance of finding a reptile or two to take back home with you as a pet. Most reptiles do not come near houses or places where there are a lot of people, but some snakes and a few lizards do. If you can go to a farm for a collecting trip or a visit, you may find corn snakes, milk snakes, rat snakes, chicken snakes, and king snakes around the barns.

As you look in the fields for snakes, lizards, or other reptiles, don't forget to look in the low trees and bushes too. Many snakes can climb very well. A few of them make their homes in trees all the time and feed on birds and other animals that also live or roost in trees. Many snakes will use trees for hiding places. Rat snakes like to climb trees and go under loose bark at night. Then they stay there until the bark is warmed by the sun the next day. If you go snake hunting in the morning, be sure to pull away large pieces

Smooth Green Snake in bush. It is easy to miss a snake sitting quietly in a bush. They usually will remain very still as you walk by. Only the bright sunlight on this specimen gave it away.

of loose bark on a tree. You may find a sleeping snake under it.

Hardware stores sell three-pronged cultivators. These are tools with long handles and three hooks on the bottom end. They make perfect reptile-hunting tools, and you should have one if you go out to hunt. Use it to turn over small logs and flat stones. Under them you are apt to find small snakes, lizards, and even turtles, which sometimes like to sleep under a flat rock that is warmed by the sunshine. In the early summer you can often find reptile eggs under the rocks, too.

You should never go looking for reptiles in the woods alone. Always take someone with you—your father, an older brother, or a friend. This is especially important if you live or hunt where poisonous snakes are known to be found. You just might be bitten by one, and your friend could help you or go for other help if he was unable to do anything himself. The chance of being bitten by a poisonous snake is very small, but it is there, and you should think about that. No chances should be taken in the woods in places where copperheads and rattlesnakes live. Never pull a log or stone with your hands. There just might be a copperhead resting underneath it. Always use your snake hook or cultivator to do the actual pulling, and always pull a rock over so you are out of the way when it falls. That way, it will not fall on your foot and hold you fast while anything underneath escapes. It just might hurt your foot, too.

Another good reason to have someone with you is that your companion can help you look for specimens. One person can pull over the log or rock and the other person can be ready to catch anything that might be underneath. But be sure that the person who is catching knows a dangerous animal when he sees one. About the only dangerous animals you might find would be copperheads and rattlesnakes, unless you live in the South and Southwest, when you could also possibly find a gila monster or coral snakes. Water moccasins are generally found not in the woods but near streams, rivers, lakes, and ponds. When you are hunting in those places, look out for them. Coral snakes usually are not easy to find. They live in burrows in the ground and seldom come out. After a rain they may be out under stones or logs, because their burrows have filled with water and they are forced to the surface. Sometimes a farmer will plow up a coral snake.

Rattlesnakes and water moccasins almost always try to escape when you come upon them in their homes. Most of the time they will slide away from you so that you will not even know they were there. Coral snakes stay in their burrows. But copperheads do not run very far. They curl up on the other side of a fallen log, under a pile of dry leaves, under a stone or piece of flat bark, and try to hide. They just sit still and you may not see them. If you step over the log you might just step right on top of one. If you do this, and you are not stepping on the snake's head, it can turn around and bite you. Always look carefully before you step over a log. It is even better not to step over the log, but to go around it to the other side. That is why it is a very good thing to look where you put your feet in the woods.

Do not step on piles of leaves or on top of pieces of fallen bark, wood, or old cardboard boxes or anything that is loose and on top of the ground. Unless you can remember to do these things it is better not to go into the woods to collect reptiles at all, but get them from a pet store.

You may find skinks out feeding in the woods. They live under logs and stones and come out to search for food among the dry leaves on the forest floor. When you hear a rustle among the leaves, remain very still. If it is a skink, you may see it after a few minutes. It will be very still itself, and it may take you several minutes to spot the animal, because it is so well hidden among the leaves. The skinks are among the fastest of all the reptiles. They drop their tails very easily, so try not to grab one by the tail. If you do, it is better to let go and allow the animal to escape than to have it lose its tail.

Many reptiles are nocturnal. Some lizards and a number

of snakes only go out at night. You might think a certain reptile is very rare because not very many of them have been found. For example, the leaf-nosed snake was thought to be one of the rarest snakes in the world because only one or two specimens were ever found. Actually it is very common. The reason not many were found was that the snake is nocturnal and only comes out at certain times during the night. When this was discovered, it was found that anybody could catch as many leaf-nosed snakes as he wanted. Now you can catch them easily at night along the road, or you can buy them from snake dealers for as little as two or three dollars!

When you find a snake, the best way to catch it is to hold it to the ground with your snake hook just behind the head. Hold it only tightly enough to keep it from running away. Too much pressure will hurt the snake, and you may even damage it severely if you are not careful. After pinning the snake to the ground with your snake hook, reach down and take hold just behind the head, and pick it up. The snake may wind itself all around your arm, but that will not hurt. Do not choke the animal. Remember that it has to breathe, so hold it just firmly enough to keep it from sliding through your hand.

The easiest way to put it into the snake sack is tail first, pushing the hand that holds the snake way down into the sack. Let go and pull your arm out of the sack quickly, and the snake is caught! Tie the neck of the sack securely in *two* places. This is not to keep the snake from escaping. If it were tied securely in one place the animal could not get away. Tying the sack in two places is to make a handle for you to carry the sack with the snake inside, without the chance of being bitten through the sack. Remember that the snake cannot hurt you very much, even if it is big enough to bite. The bite of a snake is clean and not very painful. The teeth are so sharp that they stick into you like a needle.

While I strongly recommend that you do not try to catch any poisonous snakes or lizards or try to keep them as pets, I suppose some of you will do so anyway. The double tie on the snake sack is then a perfect precaution against being bitten, but also remember that if you allow the sack to'brush against your leg while carrying it, you just might be bitten there. Also remember not to throw the sack over your shoulder to carry it, unless you happen to be wearing a suit of armor. Poisonous snakes are best put into individual sacks, then these should be placed into a carrying box or basket of some kind. This will insure you against being bitten, at least while you are carrying them home.

Catching lizards is a little harder than catching new snakes because lizards are so much faster than snakes and can hide more easily. Also, lizards can run right up a tree or a fence post or a wall and disappear before your very eyes! A good time of day to catch lizards is in the middle of the afternoon. And a good way to catch them is with a thread noose. Take a piece of buttonhole thread about a foot long and tie a loop in one end around a large nail. Make sure you tie the loop with a knot that will not slip and tighten up when you use the noose.

Cut the short end of the thread off close to the knot and slip the loop off the nail. Then put the long end of the thread through the loop to make a noose like a lasso. Tie the free end of the thread onto the end of a four- or five-foot pole. A bamboo fishing pole is perfect for this purpose. You now have a lizard noose, and you should be able to catch many animals with it.

A lizard will run a short distance when you come near, then stop and watch to see what danger is around. When it stops you can reach out slowly with the pole and dangle the noose in front of the lizard's head. Usually the animal will look at the noose but not run away from it. Slowly move the noose over the head of the reptile and as soon as it is around the neck, give a short quick jerk and you have your animal caught fast. Well, it is not caught *too* fast, because it can squirm and wiggle and slip out of the noose if you let it. But it *is* caught fast enough to let you swing it to your hands and catch hold of it to remove the noose and pop it into the catching bag. Lizards may bite when they are first caught because they have been frightened. After they are tamed they do not bite so much, but some species never get that tame. They are always afraid.

Catching lizards in the desert is different from catching them in the fields and woods. The desert lizards bury themselves under the sand and hide there. If you find any, watch them run and note where they dig under the sand. Then walk easily to the spot, reach down, and grab a handful of sand. You should have a handful of lizard too. Do not be surprised if the lizard has a mouthful of you! If it bites your hand, try not to pull your hand out of its mouth. If you do, you may possibly break its jaws. The lizard will bite for a time and then let go. Usually the bite will not even break the skin, but will just feel like a hard pinch.

When frightened, a desert lizard will try to escape to the nearest shrub or cactus. It will run up into the bush and flatten its body along the stems. When it does this, it seems to disappear. You can keep your eyes on it as it runs to the bush, then walk up and look right at it without seeing it. If there are holes around the bottom of a bush, the lizard will probably run into one of them. It is very hard to dig it out if the hole is more than a few inches deep.

Many desert lizards will run up a low sand dune and

over the top. By the time you get to the top the animal is gone. It probably ran part way down the other side and buried itself in the sand.

When you go hunting desert animals, take along a friend who can help you. When you come to a place where you see a lizard, let the friend stand at the top of a dune while you scare the lizard out. When it runs up the side of the dune, your friend can sweep loose sand down the bank in front of the lizard. The animal will keep running on the loose sand, but not get anywhere, and you can run up behind him and grab him. Catching desert lizards can be an exciting thing, and lots of fun, even if you do not bag any.

However, most of the animals that live in the desert are found only at night. They sleep during the heat of the day and come out when it is cool—in the evening and at dawn. Almost all of them are out at dawn to drink the dew on leaves and rocks. Desert animals drink when the dew or ground water rises in the early dawn. In fact, when captured, many of these lizards will not drink from a dish at all and will die of thirst in their cages. You must spray the leaves of a plant with water for them to lap up.

If it is impossible for you to go out to catch your pets, the only thing left to do is buy them in a pet store. Every city has at least one pet store, and most have several. Even in small towns there is often someone who sells animals. If the pet store does not have the kind of reptiles you want, it can get them for you. Most reptiles are fairly cheap, but some of the very rare ones can cost a lot. Snakes are the most common reptiles sold in pet stores, lizards are next, and then come turtles. Pet stores often have animals from foreign countries that would be very hard to obtain otherwise. Some of the animals from tropical countries are much more colorful than those found in this country. We have some very pretty snakes in the United States, but the tropical lizards are more highly colored and larger than the ones that live here.

Iguanas from Central America are quite common in pet stores and very reasonable in price. Most of those sold are very young babies, but often you can get some large enough so you can tell the sexes. So get a pair. Iguanas live a long time in captivity if they are cared for properly, and will become quite tame. Iguanas often can be let free in the house. They will walk around, climb up the drapes, and sit in the sun on the window sills. They will take bits of food from your hands when you go up to them. Of course, if your parents have delicate plants in the room, the iguanas might break them when they climb on them. This is not deliberate, but the animals are too heavy for such plants. They also might nibble a leaf or two, since their natural food is plants and fruits.

These lizards may get to be six feet long from the nose to the end of the tail! After they get too big for you to keep easily, you may have to sell them to someone who has more room for them. Sometimes you can donate specimens like that to small zoos or to schools. In Central and South America the people eat iguanas. The meat is supposed to taste like chicken.

The other most common lizard sold in pet stores is the little green one from the southeastern United States. It is called a chameleon, but this is not its proper name. It is not even related to the chameleon, except that both animals are lizards. The one our pet stores sell is an *anole*. The reason people keep calling it a chameleon is because the anole can change color from brown to green. A chameleon changes color too, but it has more colors than the anole.

You will probably be able to buy baby "alligators" in the pet stores. These are not real alligators, either. They are *Caymans.* Sometimes the name is spelled *Caiman.* The only trouble with caymans is that they almost always have nasty tempers and never get tame enough to handle and have fun with. Also, most of them die because they are not fed the proper food or kept at the proper temperature.

The little baby turtles you see sold for fifty cents or so are baby *slider* turtles. These are also called *red-eared* turtles, because most of them have a pretty red mark on each side of the head. When they get old they lose this pretty marking and get a lot of black stripes instead. They grow to be about six or eight inches long across the shell. Most of the food sold in pet stores for these little turtles will not keep them alive. The very worst food you can buy for them is dried ant eggs. If you feed your pet turtles dried ant eggs, the chances are that the turtles will become blind, the shells will swell or soften, and the animals will die. No matter what the pet store man tells you, dried ant eggs are poison to little turtles.

Once in a while a pet store in the bigger cities will import animals from Africa. Then you can find wonderful rare things like the Madagascan day geckos, which some people consider to be the most beautiful lizards in the world. They are bright green with orange or red marking on the back.

Tokay geckos from Malaysia are also beautiful. Some of them can be tamed, but most of them will bite you every time you pick them up. The trouble is they don't just bite you and forget about it. They keep on biting you as long as you hold them. They have really nasty dispositions. But they are so pretty and unusual that it is nice to have one. Most of the time they will feed by themselves, but some of them will not eat unless you feed them. The way to do this is to hold the gecko in your hand and wait until he tries to bite, then drop meal-worms down his mouth. He has a very big mouth, so you can drop the worms in without missing. A tokay gecko will eat twenty-five or thirty meal-worms for each meal.

The most important thing to do when buying reptiles from a pet store is to find out what the animals eat *before* you buy them. If they do not feed well, or if the clerk does not know what they eat, it is better not to buy the animal, no matter how beautiful it is, because you will not be able to keep it alive very long. If a store has a really nice animal that you want, call your zoo. Ask them if they can tell you the food and the temperature the animal needs. If you can supply these needs, then you have a good chance of keeping it contented and alive.

The many different kinds of African chameleons are wonderful to watch. But one trouble with them is that they do not live very long. Many zoos have them most of the time, but the longest they can be kept alive is about eighteen months. Perhaps the lizards are short-lived in the wild, too. Anyhow, they do not live much longer than a year or so in captivity, but while they do live they are among the most interesting pets you can possibly find. For one thing, they are not always so afraid of you that you cannot pick them up. As a matter of fact, the trouble is not picking them up but putting them down. They are difficult to get off your finger. Their feet are like tongs and they seem to want to walk only to a higher object. They rarely walk *down* off your hand.

The heads of these animals come in all shapes. Some of them have big ridges and others have horns. There are some with one horn, two horns, three horns, and even four horns on their noses! The three-horned ones look like a dinosaur called Triceratops, which lived millions of years ago.

While importing all these exotic animals from tropical countries, the pet stores may also import diseased reptiles. You should examine your animals carefully before you buy them to make sure they are healthy. Of course, if they have an internal disease you cannot tell unless the animal dies. But some diseases can be seen when a reptile is examined. Actually they are not diseases but parasites. Mites are often found on snakes and lizards. These are *arachnids* (spiders are arachnids, and so are scorpions). Some of the mites are very tiny and cannot be seen very well unless you look at the animal under a magnifying glass. If, on examination, you see these tiny parasites crawling on the animal, don't buy it. Also, make sure none of the mites come off on your hands to be put onto the next specimen you look at.

Lizards and geckos store fat in their tails. The reason for this is that, when they have a hard time finding food, they will not starve. Look at the tail of any gecko or lizard you want to buy. If it is nice and fat, the animal should be in good condition. If the tail is very skinny, it has been starved. If you starve a reptile too long, it will be unable to eat when you give it food and will die in a short time.

The next thing to look at is the skin. If the animal is fat and healthy the skin will be filled out nicely, except where it is supposed to be folded. If the skin hangs in folds and patches on the animal, it may very likely be sick.

Look carefully at the eyes of young turtles. If they are very puffy and the animal keeps them closed most of the time, you should not buy it. The chances are that the turtles have been fed on ant eggs and are going blind as a direct result of this bad food. Young turtles should be frisky and scamper all around their tank. When you see a little fellow acting like this, there is good reason to think that it is healthy and contented, and that it will feed and remain healthy as long as you take proper care of it.

Look at the skins of snakes to see if they are full of blisters and small swellings. These are generally indications of infection from ticks. Sometimes the snake will be cured when it sheds its skin. More often it will not, though, and it is not worth taking a chance.

As long as you are selecting an animal for a pet, you should take every precaution to get a healthy one to begin with. There is no sense in starting out with a specimen that is sick when you take it home.

CHAPTER 4

How to Determine a Reptile's Health

It is a good thing to know about different reptile diseases, just in case your new pet had one you did not know about when you bought it, or contracted one after you got it home. And, though humans rarely catch these diseases, it is important to identify them. There is, however, one disease that may spread to people—salmonella. This is a bad sickness, and can kill. It is sometimes given to people by pet turtles. This was not known until recently, but it has been found that small turtles (and big ones too) can carry the disease without being sick themselves. When this happens, the animal is called a carrier.

Baby turtles also frequently die from a *dietary deficiency.* This means that they are not getting the proper vitamins, minerals, and other things in their food. Such is the case when the turtle is fed dried ant eggs. It takes the turtle a long time to die, which means that it had to suffer. If your turtle shows any distress in its eyes you should make sure that you are feeding it properly. Sometimes the blindness can be treated with ultraviolet rays but the turtle does not often recover.

It is too bad that reptiles do not show signs of being

sick until they die or are ready to die. Mammals and birds show some sign of not feeling well, but not reptiles. So there is no sure way to tell whether your animal is sick when you buy it. If it dies in a short time, there is a very good chance that it was sick and nearly ready to die when you bought it.

Mites are different. These can be seen most of the time. Usually a snake or lizard does not have mites in the wild. It will have got them after it was put in the wholesale dealer's cages or in the pet store. Many thousands of animals pass through these places each year. Some of them are bound to have mites. The tiny creatures jump off the animals and live in the cages until new animals are put in with them.

The best way to examine for mites is with a strong glass in bright sunlight or a bright lamp. Look on the belly side for mites coming out from under the scutes.

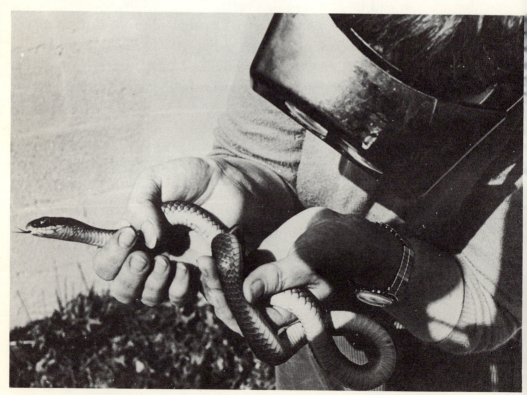

A headband magnifier is very good for detecting mites, because it leaves your hands free to hold the animal. The magnifiers come in different strengths. A good one to use for looking at animals is 10 power. Hold the lizard or snake in your hands so you can look it all over. Watch for a long time, especially at any fold in the skin. If mites are there, you will see one or more run out from under a scale and dart under another. If you see one, you may be sure there are more.

Mites are terrible for reptiles. They eat through the eyeballs into the brain and kill the animal. It is a very long and painful death. First the poor creature goes blind, then it cannot feed any more. African chameleons are the worst sufferers because their eyeballs are inside little turrets and

If your specimen is infected with mites, the best way to remove them is to hold the snake under water for several minutes. Bring its head out frequently so you do not drown him. The mites will leave the snake and drown in the water.

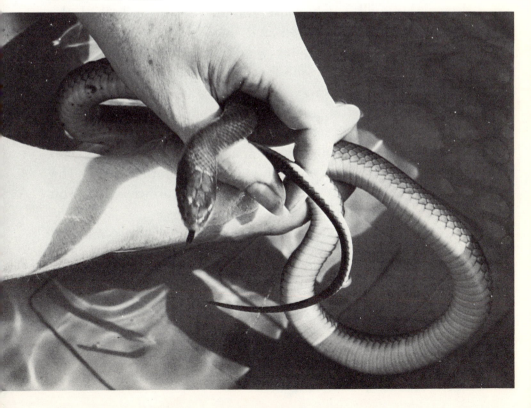

it is difficult to reach inside to get the mites out. Also, these lizards must be able to use both eyes perfectly in order to catch their food. When mites get into their eyes, there is nothing much you can do for them.

If you find mites on the skin of a reptile, put it in lukewarm water for ten to fifteen minutes at a time. Do this twice a day for two days, then once a day for a week. Then wait for three or four days and repeat the treatment. Most reptiles like water and will not struggle too much after they have been put in. Snakes will wiggle about a lot at first, then dunk themselves for a while.

You must be certain that all of the animal is under the water except the nose. The mites will drown and fall off. Remember, though, that some of them will be safe under the scales where the water will not reach, and these will not be killed. This is the reason for two baths daily for a time.

There will be eggs under the scales, too. They will not drown, but will hatch in several days. If you bathed the animal for only a few days and then left it alone, the eggs would hatch and the mites would run all over the animal again. This is why you must wait a few days and then give another week of dunking. If you do this for a month, you are pretty sure of getting rid of all the mites.

Many pet stores sell a product called Dri-Die 67. This is a powder that kills reptile mites. It would be a good idea to use the powder each day between the baths. The powder will kill any mites that did not drown when you held the reptile under water.

A good precaution to take if your animals have mites is to administer eye drops every day for a month or two. The drops can be bought in a drugstore. What you need is a .75% solution of sodium fluoride in water. This is *point 75%*, not just 75%, which would be a hundred times too strong! You might have to have your family doctor give you a prescription for the drops. He will probably do this if you tell him what you want it for.

The solution can be used to wipe the reptile's skin, too, as long as you take care not to get it in the mouth. If you see a mite duck under a scale, a drop of sodium fluoride solution can be put on that scale and the edge of the scale lifted with a pair of sharp tweezers or a toothpick to let the liquid run underneath. Just putting the solution on the scale will not do any good, because the air trapped under the scale will keep the solution from running under.

Baby iguanas need vitamins. Children's vitamins are good. A drop or two put on small pieces of lettuce will be eaten by the iguana. This should be given them every day, or at least every other day. When they get older and eat a lot of different things, the vitamins are not so important, but for the first two to three years they should have them.

Sometimes snakes will have a lot of blisters on their skins. The scales will stand up at the spot where the blisters are. Try soaking the snake in lukewarm water for ten minutes each day, and after soaking let it slide through a paper towel to dry off. Then rub a little antibiotic ointment into the blister. Neosporin or a similar preparation is good to try. The druggist will tell you of a substitute if he does not have Neosporin.

Some snakes get diseases that other snakes do not contract. The giant snakes like pythons, anacondas, and large boa constrictors might get a disease of the mouth. Mr. Raymond Ditmars, in his book *Reptiles of the World,* thinks that this disease occurs because the snake does not have enough exercise and does not feed when it is first kept captive. He says that the snake's mouth becomes stagnant and bacteria start to grow in it. Then the snake can suffer a small bruise or cut when it strikes at hard objects in the cage, or at its keeper, and the cut becomes infected.

Whatever the cause of the disease, unless it is caught very promptly and stopped, the snake will die. Mr. Ditmars suggests using Listerine. One part Listerine to two parts of boiled water should be swabbed in the snake's mouth once or twice each day. If the disease spreads, there is nothing much you can do about it. If it gets very bad, put the poor sufferer out of its misery.

The very exotic Thailand water snakes that are being imported to this country often arrive with an internal disease caused by an amoeba—a one-celled animal. The snake will die if it has the disease. There is no way you can tell whether it is present until the snake dies. The only bad thing about it is that this disease is very *contagious*. That means that, if you touch the water snake and then your other specimens, all will get it. You will not become sick, because the disease does not attack human beings. But all your other snakes and reptiles may contract it and die if the same tools or water dishes are used among your pets.

If the water snake dies and you put another reptile in the cage the water snake lived in, the new pet can also get sick and die. The only thing to do when you get one of those water snakes is to *quarantine* it. Put it into an aquarium that is kept away from all other cages or aquariums. Every time you handle anything at all connected with the water snake, you must wash your hands very well with a medicated soap. You must never use the same dish or anything at all that was in the water snake's aquarium for any other of your reptiles.

The snake should be kept in this quarantine for at least three months. Then, if it is still alive, feeding, and seems

Thailand Tentacled Water Snake. *Erpetron tentaculatum.* Actually these snakes have short fangs in the rear of the jaws, and have a mild poison. They do not harm people.

contented, you may assume that it is healthy and does not have the amoebic disease. Your precautions can then be lessened. It is still an excellent habit, though, to wash your hands well after handling any reptile before you handle the next one and after you handle the last one. The only thing that will happen to you is that you will have extra clean hands.

Big lizards that feed mostly on meat can get a vitamin deficiency disease. This will kill your pets after a time. Be sure you are feeding them properly. It is not enough to give them just bits of meat. They might eat the meat all right, but they are not getting the proper nourishment from it. Reptiles need *muscle meat.* That means things like beef heart, chicken hearts, or whole small animals like mice.

One thing that will help reptiles who are meat eaters is vitamin E. This can be given with their food.

The Cayman crocodilians are often the worst sufferers. They *must* have muscle meat in order to live, and they must be kept very warm. Not less than 80 degrees, better 85 degrees. If reptiles are kept too cold, they might eat, but they would have trouble digesting their food. It would remain in their stomachs and finally turn sour. Then the animal would get sick and eventually die.

Sometimes you will find ticks on your reptiles, especially those from pet stores, although you will also sometimes find them on wild reptiles, too. A good way to get rid of the ticks is to dab them with a cotton swab wet with a solution called A-200-Pyrinate. This can be bought in a drugstore. Be careful not to get the solution in the animal's eyes or mouth. A-200-Pyrinate might be good for mites, too, but do not cover the animal with the solution. Just put it on in spots where you know a mite is under the scale.

It is not a good idea to try to pull off ticks. The tick's head might break off and remain under the animal's skin. If this happens, the head is liable to cause an infection that is worse than the tick.

There are several other diseases that attack reptiles, but they are too hard to treat. Generally, if you keep your animals at the proper temperature, feed them the correct food and enough of it, and keep other conditions the way they like them, your reptiles will not get sick. They will live a regular life span, or sometimes even a little longer. They will be contented and not so miserable that they are always trying to escape. Many reptiles become so tame in captivity and are so contented with their food and temperature that they will not go away even if you let them out of the cage.

A snake or a lizard might suffer from a rectal plug. This means that the waste matter in the snake's intestine has hardened at the opening and the animal can no longer move its bowels. A rectal plug, or anal plug, as it is sometimes called, will kill the snake in time if it is not removed.

About the best way to open a rectal plug is to soak the animal for a period of time in tepid water. It should be in the water at least fifteen minutes or longer. Then, with a cotton swab moistened with mineral oil, gently work the plug out of the cloaca. You will be able to spread the opening enough to work the plug out. If the animal has been plugged for some time, it is very possible that when the plug is removed it will have a large bowel movement immediately. For this reason it is well to perform the service on the table on top of a thick pad of old newspaper. You might have to have a helper hold the animal while you work on it. Be very gentle and take care that you do not injure your pet.

After removing the plug, you should watch the animal closely for several days to make sure that the same thing does not happen again. If it has a bowel movement a day or so after feeding, then you can assume that it is cured and that the plug was just a temporary thing. If the animal keeps plugging up every time it feeds, then you might try changing the diet. If you were feeding one kind of food, try another and see if this clears up the trouble.

In taking care of reptiles, a lot of health measures are just plain common sense. Personal hygiene is as important to animals as it is to you. You would not keep your reptile in a dirty cage—wet, sloppy, with the waste matter not cleaned out as soon as it is made—and expect the animal to remain healthy and contented. If it spills the water out of its dish, the animal as well as the cage should be dried off. Cleanliness is the most important thing in keeping animals. Keeping some reptiles clean is a real job. They mess up their cages as fast as you can clean them. The animal is not at fault. Remember, it is not used to living in a small confined space. It is not used to having a dish of water that is easy to upset. It is forced to make adjustments. This is hard for animals, which cannot think or reason as we do. It can hardly be expected to think, "If I crawl over the edge of my water dish, the dish will tip upside down and spill all the water into my cage." You have to do this thinking for it, and fix the dish in such a way that the reptile cannot tip it over, or, if this is not possible, be prepared to clean the cage often.

Do not be unhappy that this is a chore. These are some of the things you must first take into consideration when you try to keep animals. If you want living reptiles for pets, then you must be prepared to do whatever is necessary to keep them healthy, contented, well fed, and alive.

CHAPTER 5

Kinds of Containers for Reptiles

You have brought your new pet home from the wilds, or from the pet store, and you know how to keep it well and how to cure it. Now you have to have something to keep it in. Fish aquariums make the best cages, because they are easy to clean, you can see into them, and they can be kept either warm or cool, whichever the animals need.

There are many other kinds of cages that can be used for reptiles. You can make them or have them made by a carpenter. Perhaps your father will make some for you, or help you with them. Cages for our native reptiles (except those from the deserts) should be made with a screen on the top and sides, with the back closed and a sheet of glass for the front. That way the cages will be light and airy. You can have the top hinged so it will open for cleaning or to attend to your pet. There should be a good catch on the lid to keep the reptile from forcing it open and escaping.

These kinds of cages can be made of wood and the screen can be hardware cloth with a ¼-inch mesh. This screen is strong and heavy and will not have to be protected against the animal's pushing through it. A good size cage for a medium-sized snake or lizard would be 12 or 14 inches deep, 24 inches long and 16 inches high. That would be high enough to put a small branch inside for the animal to climb on. If you were keeping an anole or chameleon the cage should be higher—24 inches or more—to allow putting in a tall branch. These lizards need to climb and like to be high up in the air.

Cages for iguanas should be even larger. These lizards must have a lot of things to climb on, because if they are unable to climb they do not remain healthy and contented. The smallest cage that is practical for iguanas would be 24 inches deep, 36 inches long and at least 36 inches high. You could, of course, keep them in a smaller cage, but they would not do so well, nor would they live so long. Iguanas grow very large, and the cage should be big enough to allow them to grow without becoming cramped. Also, iguanas are best kept in pairs for company, and the cage will have to hold two of them.

Cages for desert lizards can be low, because the animals do not have to climb. A small pile of rocks in one corner, with an opening under or between them, is all they need to climb on.

Turtles need cages that will hold some water. When turtles are small and young, the plastic dishes sold in pet stores are fine for them. As they grow larger, you will have to move them to larger cages. Many turtles need water in which to eat. Many of them cannot swallow food unless they do so *under water!* Still, even these turtles must have a place on which to climb up out of the water.

In the summer months you can keep your turtles outdoors. The large plastic pools made for babies and little children are fine turtle ponds. An island of stones can be piled in the center of the pool. Fill the pool only half way. If you put in too much water, the turtles can climb out of the pool by floating on the top and reaching up to catch the

Turtle Cage. Plastic dish with a plastic tree make a good enough cage for a baby turtle. The "tree" affords some shade from the direct rays of the sun.

edge. Always examine the pool after a rainy day, because it might fill up, if the rain is a hard one, and float the turtles close enough to the top to allow them to escape.

When the water in such pools turns green it must be changed. The green color is caused by *algae* growing in the water. The more sunshine the pool has, the faster the algae will grow. Do not wait until the water is like pea soup, but change it as soon as you notice a faint green color forming.

Outdoor cages are good for many reptiles if they come from places where the climate is the same as yours. You could not put reptiles from hot humid tropical forests outdoors, for instance, but you could keep lizards from Europe

65

and America in outdoor cages during the summer months. They will be better for having a large cage to live in, and for having regular changes of climate during the days and nights.

Outdoor cages must be absolutely tight or the animals will escape. You should never merely place the cage on top of the ground, hoping to keep your pet inside. Within minutes, probably, the animal will have seen a hole that you didn't even know was there to scoot out through.

The very best way to set up an outdoor cage is to put a footing into the ground, on top of which you can fasten the cage. The footing could be located in an out-of-the-way spot in the back yard. It should be not less than 1 foot deep in the ground, and it would be better if it went down 2 feet.

The footing can be made of many materials. The best and the easiest to maintain is concrete. Dig a ditch the size of the cage and 1 to 2 feet deep. The ditch should be about 6 inches wide. You can mix some concrete in an old tub or a wheelbarrow and pour it into the ditch until it is filled to ground level.

If the ground in your yard is uneven, then a form must be made in the ditch to get the top of the footing level. The form can be two boards stood on edge in the ditch and raised or lowered until the top edges are all the same height and all level. An ordinary carpenter's level can be used to set the form boards. The boards can be held in place by a small stake driven into the ground on the outside of the form and the board nailed to the stake. Your father, older brother, or friend could help you make the form and the ditch. They could also help you mix and pour the concrete.

When the concrete has been poured into the ditch, you can set two steel bolts into each side. Set them about a foot from each end and leave about 3 inches sticking out of the concrete. The head end of the bolt should be put down into the cement. Then, when the footings are hard, the cage can be bolted down tightly to the level concrete and the animals will be unable to dig from under the sides.

A cage for snakes does not have to be covered if the sides are made high enough. The longest snake you will be keeping inside the cage should be measured, and the height of the sides should be one and a half times the length of the snake. This way the snake cannot work its way up in a corner far enough to get its head on top. If a snake can reach the top of a cage with its head, it can hook its chin over the edge and pull its entire body up to escape.

Cages for lizards must be covered, because they can climb right up the screen or the corners. Geckos can walk up the sides even if they are made of glass. In a closed cage, there must be some way for you to feed and water the animals. The top can be made so it can be removed when you want to reach inside. This is easier than trying to make a door that is tight enough to keep the animals from escaping.

CHAPTER 6

Maintenance of Reptiles in Cages

In order to keep reptiles, you must have proper cages for them to live in. The last chapter dealt with the *kinds* of cages needed. This chapter will explain what you must have *inside* the cages.

Cages for reptile pets can be divided into several classes: hot, cool, moist, dry, and combinations of all of these. For desert reptiles, cages should be hot and dry. For forest reptiles, cages should be cool and moist. Tropical reptiles are healthiest when their cages are hot and damp. Sometimes it is not possible for you to maintain a cage with the proper conditions for a certain reptile. If that is the case, then it would be best if you did not try to keep that kind of animal. It would only sicken and die.

To set up a cage for a baby cayman, you should first find out as much about caymans as you possibly can. Read about them in the chapter on lizards in this book. Ask your pet store dealer to tell you all he knows about keeping a cayman. If your city has a zoo, the keeper there should be glad to give you whatever information he has. You will find that caymans need water to swim in. They need a dry place where they can get out of the water. They also need room to move about when they feed. They need a warm cage—80 to 85 degrees at the least, but not above 90 degrees.

With all this information, it should be easy to make a very nice home for a baby cayman out of a tropical fish aquarium. Aquariums used to cost a lot of money but today you can buy a nice big one for a few dollars. The aquarium for a cayman should be not less than 20 gallons, but a bigger one would be better—as big as you can afford to buy. After getting the aquarium, hunt in a field for some nice flat rocks. They should not be too big, but you do not want tiny ones either. Ones about the size of a saucer are fine.

You should get enough of these flat rocks to make a pile about one third of the way up the aquarium, clear across one end and part way down one side. Stack them one on top of the other, making sure that you stack them in such a way that they will not topple over. The top layer should be as level as you can make it and should hang over the edge of the rocks for a few inches, to make a ledge out over the water.

Put the aquarium in a permanent place near a window where it will get some sunlight each day, but not the direct rays of the sun. It should be on a strong steady support, because when the water is in the cage it will be very heavy. Add water to the aquarium until the level is just below the tops of the rocks.

Now you must have a small aquarium heater, with a thermostat installed in it. Set the thermostat to 85 degrees and slip the heater down in one corner of the aquarium. If you can get it in the corner behind the rocks it would be best. Then the cayman cannot get at the heater and accidentally change the setting. The heater must be completely under the water or it will burn out. These small aquarium heaters are not designed to work in air—only in water.

In a ten-cent store you can find small growing plants. You should get one or two of these. The ones with the big leaves are best. They are called *philodendrons,* and they are very cheap. Put the potted plants in the corner on top of the rocks. Arrange the leaves of the plants to make a dense bunch in the corner. Hang an aquarium thermometer in the tank so that you can see the scale when you look through the front glass. A sheet of glass to cover the aquarium should be obtained and put on top to close it.

Cut off a triangle from one corner of the glass to allow the heater cord to pass through. This will also let air enter the tank so the cayman can breathe. Allow the cage to stand for at least two days until the water temperature and air temperature are almost equal. Watch the thermometer. The air temperature should be between 80 and 85 degrees. The water can be a little bit less. Now put in the cayman. Watch it for a while. It should remain active and alert. If it does, the conditions are right. Do not put more than one animal in a small aquarium. If the cage is big enough, two caymans can be kept together, but they should be the same size. All reptiles will fight each other if they are different sizes. The big ones will pick on the little ones and may even eat them.

A cage for desert animals is much different from one for animals that live in water or in humid conditions. It is more difficult to keep a desert cage warm enough, because air heaters are sometimes very expensive to buy, and it would cost too much to set up a cage with a thermostat control for one or two desert animals. One way such a cage can be kept warm enough is to use a short water-pipe heater buried in the sand. These heaters are flat wires that are plugged into an electrical outlet. They come in many different lengths. The short 3- or 4-foot ones are best. Some of them have built-in thermostats, and others are plain. The plain ones are best for heating a cage.

For a desert lizard or other desert animal, you should put in two or three inches of clean sand or fine aquarium gravel. A heater wire can be buried in the sand, but not less than an inch below the surface. Bend the wire in zigzags across the tank, but be sure that you do not bend it so that it crosses itself at any spot. If a pipe-heater wire is crossed over itself, it may burn out at that point. It will get too hot where the two loops touch. Bring the plug end of the heater wire up one corner of the cage, so you can plug it into an extension cord for electrical current.

A few small cacti or succulent plants can be bedded in the sand to the level of the top of the pots. There is no need to put in a water dish, because practically no desert animals drink out of a standing supply of water. They drink only dew on the leaves at night or in the early morning. Make your cage setup so you can remove part of the lid to water the pets properly. Water should be sprayed on the plants until drops are left standing. This should be done each morning and each night.

Soon the animals will learn where their water is, and walk over to lick up the "dew-" drops. Be careful when you spray the water so you will not get too much water in the cage. You should try not to wet the sand. If the plants are all placed in the same corner of the cage, when you water them the rest of the cage will remain dry and warm. The animals will move away from the damp sand around the plants after they have drunk, and go back to where it is dry.

Lizards native to the forests need cages that are dry and a little cool. They also need a lot of leaves or other forest debris on the bottom of their cages and a small dead log or branch on which to climb. Many forest lizards can drink from a water dish. If you are not sure of the drinking habits of any animal you are keeping, always put in a small dish of water and watch the pet very closely for a few days to see if it drinks. You must be sure that the animal is really drinking, not just smelling the water.

If you see it actually drink from the dish, then you can keep a small dish of water in the cage all the time. Change the water every day. If, after a couple of days, you see that the animal is not drinking from the dish, put a plant with broad leaves (such as a small philodendron) in the cage and spray the leaves well. If the reptile is a dewdrop drinker, it will usually run right over to the plant and begin licking up the drops. If this is what happens, you must water the plant by spraying at least twice every day.

In a forest cage, it doesn't matter if a little water sprays on the dead leaves on the bottom. Leaves in the forest are usually a little damp anyway, and it will not hurt the animals; however, the bottom should not be soaking. You can put some dirt in the bottom of a forest cage if you like, but it should be very clean sterilized soil.

You can buy small bags of sterile potting soil in most supermarkets and nurseries. Then you mix it with an equal amount of sand. The sand should be cleaned by washing it very well in a pan, then spreading it on a flat pan and baking it in the oven until it is dry. Spread the mixture of soil and sand on the bottom of the cage, then cover the soil with the dead leaves. Collect nice clean leaves from under a tree, or from the forest. Examine all the leaves to make sure that there are no spiders, insects, or dirt on them before using them in the cage. A small rock or two and a small log or branch will be welcomed by your pets.

The most important thing to remember when setting up a cage for a reptile is to make it as nearly like the natural habitat as possible. Of course the exact conditions cannot be duplicated. You can, however, make it enough like a natural spot that the animal will be contented and stay healthy.

CHAPTER 7

Reptile Food and How to Grow It

Almost all reptiles eat meat—other animals or insects. A few lizards and turtles are *vegetarians*—that is, they eat fruit and vegetables instead of meat. Vegetarian reptiles are the easiest to keep and feed. There is no problem about finding food during the winter months, because lettuce, carrots, and some kinds of fruit are always available. Canned fruit salad, with the juice drained off, is good food for many vegetarian lizards, like the iguanas, which will eat this during the winter.

To keep the meat eaters that do not hibernate alive through the winter, you must be able to find the proper kinds of food. If they are insect feeders, it is possible to buy crickets and meal-worms. There are several companies in the United States that sell crickets by the hundreds or thousands as fishing bait. These companies generally place ads in sporting magazines. Look in the classified ad pages. Meal-worms are the larvae of a small beetle. Most pet stores sell meal-worms for about a penny each, or a little cheaper by the hundred. Some larger pet stores sell them by the quarter- or half-pound.

You may have to grow food for your reptiles. This is not as hard as you may think, even if it is a bit of a nuisance. Meal-worms, crickets, grasshoppers, and earthworms can be raised successfully through the winter.

Meal-worm "farms" can be set up with very little trouble.

You will need to set up three farms. Variety stores, department stores, and discount stores all sell large plastic boxes. One very common size is about 11 inches wide, 16 inches long and 4 inches deep. This size is perfect for a meal-worm farm. First you should bore holes through the top. If you use a small drill, about ⅛ inch in diameter, bore several dozen holes. Make regular rows all the way down or across the top. The beetles will not be able to climb through a ⅛-inch hole, but the insects will get enough air through the holes.

A meal-worm "farm." Plastic boxes with holes cut into the lids and screen fastened over the holes make good places to raise meal-worms.

Cut four to six pieces of burlap just large enough to cover the bottom of the plastic box. You can now set up your first farm. Sprinkle a handful of oatmeal, corn meal, or almost any dry cereal on the bottom of the box. Lay three or four thin slices of apple or raw potato on top of the cereal, then drop in a small handful of meal-worms.) (You should start with not less than a quarter-pound of meal-worms when setting up a breeding farm.) Cover the worms with a sheet of burlap. Now repeat the process . . . Sprinkle a good handful of cereal on the burlap, a few slices of potato or apple, and a few dozen more worms, laying another sheet of burlap on top. Make four to six layers like this, then put the lid on the box and put it in a warm dry location. You do not need sunlight. In fact, it is better if the box is kept in the dark.

Meal-worms go through a complete metamorphosis in their life history. A complete metamorphosis means that the insect starts as an egg. The egg hatches into a larva. (The meal-worms are larvae.) The larva turns into a pupa. Some insects spend the winter as the pupa, coming out in the spring as the adult.

Meal-worms, however, are *continuously brooded*. This means that they have many generations through the year, instead of only one or two. The meal-worm that hatches from the egg grows until it is about an inch long. It sheds its skin several times during this period. The pupa remains still for a few days, and finally the skin splits on the back and the adult beetle emerges.

Meal-worm beetles do not fly, they just crawl around the box until they find a mate. They lay their eggs in the fibers of the burlap and on dried, partly eaten slices of potato and apple, then die. Most reptiles will not eat the beetle stage of meal-worms. Several days after the eggs are laid, they start to hatch into tiny meal-worms. These are so small you can hardly see them with the naked eye. In a few days they are nice small worms and from that time they grow rapidly. The potato and apple slices are put in the farms to provide moisture for the worms, and you will see them gather all around the slices, nibbling at them. When almost all the slices are eaten or dried up, you should put in fresh ones. Put some in each layer, but do not throw out the old ones, because these can be full of eggs. Never dampen the cereal or keep the farm in a damp place. Meal-worms *must* be kept dry at all times.

A few weeks after setting up your farm, you will see a few beetles in among the layers. They are about half an inch long, and they may be brown, black, or pale tan. This is the time to set up farm number two. The worms in farm number one are starting to turn into beetles. This means that you should not use them for food any more, but let them rest and lay their eggs for the new crop. When farm number two starts to produce beetles, set up farm number three. When farm number three shows beetles crawling around, you should have nice plump worms in farm number one, and you can start feeding from that one again. From now on, the farms should rotate so you will always have a good supply of worms to feed your pets. Just keep feeding from them in order, letting the other two breed or grow.

Cricket farms are a little harder to keep, but they should be made too, in order for you to have a change of food for your reptile pets. One of the large plastic or galvanized garbage cans makes a good cricket farm. Put three or four inches of dirt mixed with a little sand in the bottom of the can. You do not need a lid, because crickets cannot jump out of the large-sized cans. A few rocks should be placed on top of the dirt, because crickets go under rocks to hide. Now add some dead leaves.

Crickets will eat almost any vegetable or fruit. The food should be put into a shallow pie plate or on a flat rock. Do not dump it on the dirt. Water should be sprinkled on the dead leaves at least once a day, and the dirt should be kept very slightly damp at all times, but never actually wet. Give your crickets meat scraps from the table. If they do not have meat fed to them, they will become cannibals and eat each other.

Cricket farms can be kept in the cellar where it is cool and dark. They do not need sunlight, although a little sunshine each day will not hurt them. The thing to remember about a cricket farm is that they chirp most of the time. Unless you keep the farm in some out-of-the-way place, the chirping may bother your family at night. Crickets need a lot of food, so you must be careful to see that they do not run short.

Grasshoppers are kept just like crickets, except that you must make a screen cover for the garbage cans, because grasshoppers can jump higher than crickets. They can also climb up the sides of the can. Grasshoppers eat the same things that crickets do, and need water sprinkled on the soil and leaves, too. Grasshoppers are harder to raise than crickets. They often are attacked by a threadworm that kills off the entire farm. But if you keep the can clean, feed them well, and do not let food rot in their cage you should not have too much trouble.

Earthworms can be raised in farms. They need damp soil no less than a foot deep. Rich woods soil is the best, with plenty of rotting leaf mold in it. A piece of bread moistened with milk may be laid on the surface of the soil to provide food for the worms. As this disappears, it can be replaced with a fresh piece. Do not let the bread get sour and start to decay. Then the soil will get sour and the worms will die.

Magazines have ads for worm cultures for setting up your worm farm. These worms are sold with a sheet of instructions. You should read them, because each species of worm should be treated differently. Dry corn meal sprinkled on the surface of the soil will be eaten by worms. They like it damp and cool. The cellar is the best place for a worm farm. Earthworms are excellent food for small snakes, and especially for garter snakes. If you want to keep a snake active through the winter, a worm farm will provide you with enough food to do so.

Other insects can be raised without too much trouble; however, your parents might not like to have some of them around. Roaches and flies are easy to raise, but if they escape in the house your mother might stop your farming activities. Aphids are good food for small lizards like anoles. They love to eat aphids, those small insects that suck the juice from plants, and will eat them right off the twig the insects live on. In the fall you should go out to look for colonies of aphids. Look on the younger branches of trees and shrubs, on the stems of flower plants and ornamental plants.

In order to keep aphids inside you need growing plants that are *succulent* or plants that have a lot of sap in their stems. Geraniums are good. Philodendrons and nephthytis are also good. These plants should be kept in a place where the aphids can be confined. If you do not protect the plants, the aphids will spread to your mother's house plants.

A good way to set up an aphid farm is to get an aquarium large enough to hold several plants in pots. The aquarium must also be large enough to allow the stems of the plants to stand up inside without touching the top. A sheet of glass is put on top of the aquarium to keep the aphids from wandering.

After you have put several growing plants in the aquarium, snip off a twig with a small colony of aphids from a flower or plant outside, and put it in among the leaves of your farm plants. The aphids will eventually migrate to the stems of your plants and the farm is all set.

When you see good colonies of aphids collected on the stems of your plants you can either snip off small sections with the insects on them and put them into the anole cage, or you can put your anole into the aphid farm for an hour or two and let it feed directly off the farm plants. Then you can return it to its own cage. The lizard should be fed once every day or so. Be sure, however, you use only plain green aphids. There is another type called woolly aphids but lizards do not seem to like them so well.

Spiders are a choice bit of food for small lizards. They can be raised, but it is hardly necessary, because you can always find one or two around the house. Look in dark corners in the cellar, on stairs, in the attic. The only trouble with raising spiders as food for lizards is that you have to feed the spiders, too. This defeats your purpose because spiders are also meat-eating animals.

When you have young reptiles like lizards and anoles, or maybe young geckos, it is hard to find insect food small enough for them to eat. Fruit flies are good for this purpose. They are very easy to raise in "fly farms" and they are a perfect size for tiny reptiles.

Miss Alice Gray of the American Museum of Natural History has given me the recipe for food on which to raise fruit flies. It was invented by *entomologists* at Columbia University. Entomologists are people who study insects. Empty instant coffee jars (the large size) make excellent fruit-fly

81

farms. The recipe below will make enough food for about
four jars:

Water	¾ cup
Molasses	1½ tablespoons
Salt	1 pinch
Cream of Wheat	2½ tablespoons
Dry Yeast	1 package

Bring the water, molasses, and salt to a boil in a saucepan,
then sprinkle the Cream of Wheat slowly into the water,
stirring all the time. Cook until the cereal begins to thicken.
Pour it at once into the bottom of the jars, an equal amount
in each jar. Sprinkle ¼ package of dry powdered yeast
into each jar before the mush hardens. Fold a paper towel
into several thicknesses and stick it down into the mush, then
allow the jars to cool and set.

You can buy cultures of fruit flies from companies that
sell supplies to schools. Possibly your science teacher can
get you a start of flies. If the climate is warm enough, just
putting out a piece of ripe melon, banana, or other soft fruit
will attract fruit flies from the wild, and you can use these to
"seed" your farm. Put a dozen or more fruit flies into each
jar, covering the tops with a piece of very fine material. A
square of an old sheet or pillowcase will do, or use an old
handkerchief or several thicknesses of cheesecloth. You must
use at least three or four thicknesses of material if you use
cheesecloth, because the fruit flies will climb out through
the mesh of one or two layers.

Put your farms in a warm dry place for several days. The
flies will mate and lay eggs on the mush. When the eggs
hatch, the maggots will eat the mush until they grow large
enough to make their pupae. They will then climb up the
paper towel to pupate. Many will also pupate on the sides of

the jar. A few days after the pupae appear, the flies will emerge from them and start flying around inside the jar. When you see a lot of flies buzzing around, you can start using them for food for your young animals. Each jar should last you for several days. Just before all are gone, you should start new farms in fresh jars. By maintaining fresh farms, you can keep a steady supply of fruit flies growing while your animals are feeding on them.

Sometimes you have baby animals when you cannot get food for them. African animals and those from below the equator have often mated already when the pet stores get them for sale here. Spring in these places is autumn where we are, so in our fall or early winter the tropical pet will surprise you by having its young just when all your food supply is gone because of the cold.

If you have such reptiles for pets, even though you are not sure what sex your pet is, it would be an excellent idea to start some fruit-fly farms in the late summer, just in case. Nothing but a little time and trouble will be lost if your pet does not have any young, but having a few fruit-fly farms producing may mean the difference between keeping the young alive and watching them starve to death if you *don't* have farms ready.

Each time a farm begins to have a large fly population, make up four more jars and "seed" them from the first ones. This way, the flies will be growing steadily all through the fall and winter. As the farm grows, the flies will die off if they are not needed for food, but if young animals are born, you will not be taken by surprise and you will be able to feed them through the winter months.

If your reptiles feed on mice or other small mammals, you can buy or raise white mice. Guinea pigs and rabbits can also be kept for larger reptiles. Almost any reptile that has a large enough mouth will eat small mice. There are two stages of young mice that can be used as food for reptiles. The first are "pink mice." Pink mice are the tiny babies that have just been born. These are small enough to feed medium-sized lizards. Larger chameleons will also eat pink mice, as will tokay geckos.

The next stage of mammal food for reptiles is "weaners." These are young mice that have just been weaned by their mothers. They have their fur and their eyes are open. They are good for young caymans and large lizards and for medium-sized snakes. Full-grown mice are used for snakes, caymans, and very large carnivorous lizards.

Keeping white mice is easy enough if you have the space for it, and if you keep them spotlessly clean. If you do not, they smell. No parent will allow a smelly mouse cage around the house. To start a mouse "farm" all you need are two females and one male. They mate and breed regularly, and the females have several young at one time. Naturally, the best time for a mouse farm is in the winter when it is difficult to find food for your pets. If you cannot keep mice yourself, the next best thing is to buy them. There are many wholesale mouse breeders in the country. They make a big business out of raising mice for hospitals, schools, and laboratories. If you are fortunate enough to live near enough to one of these companies, you can usually buy mice rejects from them for just a few cents each. Often they will sell you a whole bunch of pink mice or weaners for practically nothing. If you cannot find a breeder, then try a pet store.

Almost any boy knows how to raise rabbits and guinea pigs. If you have a large snake like a young python or big boa constrictor, small rabbits or guinea pigs make good food. When your cayman gets bigger, it will also eat these things.

At any time you can catch birds for your larger reptiles,

such as some of the snakes. It is very easy to trap live sparrows in the summer and juncos in the winter. Just prop a box up with a stick under one edge. Tie a long string to the stick and lead it inside through the window or door. Scatter a handful of wild bird seed, bread crumbs, or dry cereal under the box and sit down for a few minutes. Soon there will be a number of birds pecking away at the bait. Slowly and gently pull the string until the stick falls away from the box. The chances are that you will have more than one bird each time you spring the trap!

CHAPTER 8

Winter Maintenance of Reptile Pets

Some reptiles can be forced to hibernate through the winter months. Those that come from this country where the winters are cold are easy to hibernate. Some of the reptiles from Europe can also be kept this way—especially if they are from that part of Europe that has the same kind of climate we have. Just about all you need for this is a few unbleached muslin bags and permission from your parents to use a small space in the refrigerator.

A snake or lizard to be hibernated is put into a bag and the opening tied very securely in *two* places, about an inch apart. The bag is placed in a back corner of the refrigerator where it will be out of the way and not liable to have a heavy bowl of leftovers plopped on top of it. The time to do this is when you cannot get any more live food for the animal, or when the frost starts to get heavy in the evening or morning.

After putting the animal away, examine it about once a week to make sure it is healthy and contented. If it was well fed and healthy when you started to hibernate it, there should be no trouble. If you can find a bit of food for it, it will not hurt to take it out, let it warm up and feed. Wait a day or so until it gets rid of its waste matter, then put it back in the bag and cool it again.

As the winter progresses, you can take it out less often. In the middle of the winter once every two weeks should be enough. When it is really deep winter, once a month should be all right. Each time you take the animal out of the cold and let it warm up, you should let it have a drink of water. When it stops drinking, you can dip it in tepid water for a few minutes to let it soak. Then it can go back in the bag and the refrigerator, but only after you dry it off.

Reptiles can be overwintered outside, too. This is harder to do than putting them in bags. The reason it is harder is that you have to make a place for them that will protect them from freezing. You also have to protect them from enemies. A good method of hibernating snakes outside is to dig a hole and fill it with rocks. The hole should be at least two feet deep, and deeper if possible, if your area has a deeper frost line. The bottom should be filled with small cracked rocks or large pebbles to a depth of not less than six inches. This is to form a drain so that, when it rains, the animal will not drown if it is resting in the bottom of the hole. On top of the cracked rocks, pile large stones close together until the hole is filled. Then continue to pile the stones until you have a high mound of them on top of the hole. Make sure there are spaces between the stones through which your animal will be able to crawl.

When the hole is made and filled, you must put a cage around it to keep your animal from wandering off and to keep enemies out. A few weeks before it is time to go to bed for the winter you can put your pet in his outdoor cage, which may be called a *hibernaculum*. A hibernaculum is a place where an animal or insect can hibernate for the winter. Feed your pet a few times in the new cage, and when it gets too cold for the animal, it will crawl down into the pile of rocks for protection. The rocks hold the heat of the sun. At the bottom of the hole it will remain a little above freezing.

The animal will survive, although it will become stiff and cold and will not move.

If a long warm spell comes in the middle of the winter, the rocks may warm up enough to awaken the snake and it may crawl out to sun itself on top of the rock pile. As soon as the sun goes down in the afternoon it will go back under the rocks. You do not need to examine the animal the way you do when you have it indoors. Rain, dew, or melting snow will provide enough water for it, and it will not have to be soaked because it will never completely dry out the way it would in the refrigerator.

Turtles may be kept through the winter by making a pen out of four one-foot-wide boards set on the ground. Put the turtle inside and fill the enclosure up with hay. Pack the hay nicely into the pen so the space is well filled. The turtle will dig under the surface of the ground and the hay on top will keep it from freezing. Most turtles, however, do not need to be hibernated, because they eat dead meat and vegetables. As long as you do not have to provide living food for it, an animal can be kept active in the winter.

Tropical reptiles can neither be put into the refrigerator nor hibernated outdoors since they do not hibernate in their natural habitat. In the cold of our climate they are apt to catch pneumonia and die before the winter is over. A tropical reptile must be kept warm and fed through the winter. It may not need *much* food, but it does need some, and this should be considered when you buy such a pet—how will you be able to feed it in the winter? If there is any doubt in your mind that you will be able to feed it through the long winter months, you should not get the animal, because it will only suffer, and will probably die.

As winter progresses, some animals will stop feeding. You may not notice this for some time, but finally you will realize that your pet has not been eating all the food you have been putting in its cage. Each day it eats less and less. Finally it stops eating almost entirely. What is happening is that the animal is following an instinctive pattern in its life. It ate a lot of food right up to the fall or early winter days, and stored up a lot of fat in its body. If it is a lizard or gecko, most likely the fat was stored in its tail. Then, when the normal time came for it to hibernate in its natural habitat, it stopped feeding and became very quiet in the cage. Even though it is kept warm and food is available, the instinct is so strong that the animal obeys the pattern.

If this happens, do not worry about your pet starving to death. It is living off the stored fat in its body. Since the animal does not move about very much, it does not need much energy to remain healthy. Just the same, you should offer food every few days, to see if it is taken. Do not allow the food to remain in the cage until it dies or goes bad. If the pet does not feed within a reasonable time, remove the food and try again in another few days. You should always have water available, however.

During this period of normal inactivity, it would be best if you did not handle your pet very much. First of all, it is in a somewhat dormant state, and it is more insensible to your handling. Next, it may very probably disturb the normal functions of its body to be handled during a time when usually it would be completely inactive. Look at it in its cage, but do not take it out to play with it until you see it becoming active of its own accord. When this happens, start feeding it again on its regular schedule.

You should always try to keep different kinds of reptiles in different cages, by themselves. If you cannot do this, and one of them tries to go into hibernation, you should take the others out and put them in a separate cage so the hibernating animal can be alone.

CHAPTER 9

The Best Kinds of Snakes
to Keep as Pets

Not every snake will make a good pet. Some of them will not even live in captivity. Some of them will refuse to feed. Others are so easily frightened that they become frantic whenever anyone approaches the cage. I have seen many snakes with sore, bloody noses. They got that way from dashing against the glass trying to escape whenever a person went near them. These kinds of snakes are not good animals to try to keep as pets. Actually, they never become pets, but are merely captive animals. They are miserable, and most of the time do not live very long.

The kinds of snakes you want to keep as pets are those that live well in a cage—the kinds that will let you pick them up and handle them without going mad with fear, the kinds that will curl up contentedly in your lap while you stroke their bellies or backs, and seem to enjoy such treatment, the kinds that will feed out of your hand or at least let you watch them eat.

Many different species of these kinds of snakes are to be found. As we have mentioned in previous chapters, before you select your pet snake, find out what it feeds on, if you can keep it alive through the winter, if you can find food for

Thamnophis sirtalis. After a few days of kind handling, garter snakes learn they have nothing to be afraid of, and from then on will tame up very quickly, eat out of your hands, and make no attempt to escape when taken from their cages.

it without too much trouble or expense and if you can provide proper accommodations for it.

Snakes can be divided roughly into four groups. (1) Those from the Temperate Zones of the world. (2) Those from deserts. (3) Those from the tropics. And (4) a special group called exotic snakes.

Temperate Zone snakes come from the United States, from most of Europe, and a few other places. These snakes can withstand our climate. They generally hibernate during the winter. They do not require special temperatures or conditions of humidity in their cages. And, what is more important, they are readily available in pet stores, they are low priced, and, in many cases, you can catch them yourself.

About the easiest kind of snake to feed is one that eats small rodents and mammals. These are easiest because you can always get food for them in the form of white mice from a pet store. You can also raise the mice yourself if you want to.

Mammal feeders are also the easiest kinds of snakes, other than garter snakes, to find in pet stores. Some snakes that feed on small animals do not make good pets because they never become tame enough. Others live very well in cages and seem to like being handled and played with. They become very tame and do not even try to escape when you let them out of their cages. Of course, any snake will crawl away and escape if you allow it to. Sometimes it is not trying to escape from you but crawls into a hole or a place where you cannot get it back. The result is the same as though it had run from you.

King snakes are about the best mammal eaters you could find to keep as pets. In our country there are several kinds of king snakes. Then there are several kinds of snakes that belong to the king-snake group but are called by other names. The true king snakes belong to the genus *Lampropeltis*. *Lampropeltis* means "shiny skin," and the king snakes have smooth scales and a shiny surface. They are among the most beautiful of all snakes. King snakes are called that because of their ability to kill and eat other snakes. They can kill poisonous snakes such as rattlesnakes and copperheads. They can even let themselves be bitten by rattlesnakes and the venom does not harm them if the bite is not in a critical spot.

The king snake is a constrictor and usually eats small mammals. Because of this, its teeth are very long and it can bite. This very seldom happens, 'however, since it is difficult to get some king snakes to open their mouths unless they are feeding or drinking. Unless the snake is after food, it does not move very fast. It likes to lie curled up in a corner; sometimes it stays curled up in its water dish, soaking. When you handle your king snake, let it wrap its body around your arm or around your hand. It will hang on tightly, and seems to have a feeling of security if it has a good hold on you. It will remain quiet and calm and you can examine it as long as you like. A good way to hold a king snake is to hold up one hand with your fingers spread wide apart. The snake will wind in and out of your fingers until it is tied in' a knot all around your hand. Then it will stay quietly and you can carry it around.

Never, NEVER put a king snake or any constrictor around your neck. While other snakes can be draped over your shoulders or around your neck, it is most foolhardy to do this with a constrictor. If you have a large king snake it is a good idea always to have a friend with you when you take it out of the cage to examine or play with. The natural thing for a constricting snake to do is tighten up around anything it is resting on. If you drape it over your shoulders, there is a good chance that it will wind around your neck and tighten up.

A good-sized king snake or other kind of constrictor can really exert a lot of pressure. It is not trying to hurt you, but just the same, it could tighten up around your neck and strangle you. It would be very hard for you to get such a snake off your neck. The more you pulled at it, trying to loosen its coils, the more it would tighten up to hold on. It is almost impossible to unwind a constrictor snake from the head backward. It is easier to do so from the tail forward, but if the snake were around your own neck, you might not be able to see what you had to do in time to keep from being choked to death!

Speckled King Snake. *Lampropeltis getulus holbrooki*. The easiest way to hold a king snake is to spread your fingers and let the animal tie itself into a knot on your hand. They have a very strong grip.

There is no danger in handling a king snake if you do not put it around your neck. It cannot hurt you around your waist, for instance, or around your arm or leg. So you do not have to be afraid to keep a king snake as a pet. They are among the best kinds for this purpose. As I mentioned before, there are several kinds of king snakes in this country. There are also a few species that live in the tropics down as far as Ecuador.

Many king snakes are just *subspecies*. This means that there might be a race of snakes with a different patch of color, or some other very slight difference from the usual snake of this species. If this happens, the snake is given three names instead of only two, and it is said to belong to a subspecies. We are not interested in this fine a division of snakes. In keeping pets, knowing the species is enough. Sometimes a race of slightly different snakes is found only in a very limited area of the country, and its third name is taken from that location. The three main kinds of king snakes are the common king snake, the Eastern king snake, and the Southern king snake. Each has several subspecies, but they are, as I said, merely local varieties of the same species.

The common king snake is glossy black with large cream blotches all over the back, sides, and belly. The adult length is about four feet but specimens as long as six feet ten inches are on record. The common king snake is found almost everywhere in the United States. Wild specimens may be found under rotting logs, stones, old lumber. They are fond of sunning themselves in the morning and early afternoon. In the hot summer they are out more at night than in the daytime. When first caught, they might strike at you, hiss, and vibrate their tails, but they become tame almost immediately and rarely, if ever, bite.

The Eastern king snake is a beautiful glossy black snake

King Snake. *Lampropeltis getulus.* One of the most gentle of all snakes, this one will attack, kill and eat a rattler as large as itself!

with narrow cream-colored bands running around the body. It can be found in the southern states and the eastern states, west to the Appalachians. The Southern king snake is covered with white or yellow spots all over its body. It is sometimes called the salt-and-pepper snake or speckled king snake. It can be found over the southeastern section of the United States.

King snakes will eat other things besides mice. In the summer, when frogs and salamanders are plentiful, they will devour them. They may eat other snakes, lizards, or small birds when available.

The milk snake is really a king snake. The animal is called a milk snake for a very silly reason. Milk snakes very often go into barns where cows are kept. They look for mice that live among the hay and straw in cow barns. Years ago, if a farmer found a milk snake in his barn he thought it wanted to suck the milk from his cows. The story is not true, but it is how the milk snake got its name.

These beautiful snakes are about three feet long. They are light gray with chestnut-brown or reddish markings on the back. They are found over almost the entire United States. Sometimes they are called house snakes, checkered adders, or spotted adders. They are easy to tame and live well in captivity.

The rat snakes, like the king snakes, are constrictors. They feed on rodents, birds, and sometimes frogs. Rat snakes are also called chicken snakes. This is because they are often found around chicken houses. They might eat a baby chick once in a while, but the real reason they hang around chicken houses is the same reason milk snakes hang around barns—they are looking for rats and mice, both of which live in large numbers in barns and poultry houses.

One type of rat snake is even more beautiful than the milk snake. This is the one called the red rat snake. It is also called the corn snake because it is often seen in cornfields. It is looking for the field mice that build their nests in the rubble in cornfields. Corn snakes are cream, gray, or pale red with dark red, brown, or chestnut markings on the back and belly. They have a beautiful play of color on their belly scales.

The green rat snake comes from Mexico and is grayish green on the back with the scales tipped in black. The belly is white. There are several species of rat snakes, and they are found all over the country. Rat snakes can be found under

Corn Snake (*Elaphe g. guttata*) in weeds and grass. Even though you know the snake is there, if you look at it long enough and let your eyes go slightly out of focus the animal will seem to disappear.

large pieces of loose bark on dead trees. In the morning or evening they like to go under the bark where it is warm. Rat snakes are very good climbers and spend a lot of time in trees.

Rat snakes, chicken snakes, and pilot black snakes all belong to the group called *Elaphe*. Pilot black snakes are so named because at one time people wrongly thought they led rattlesnakes and copperheads to safety when any of them were in danger of being caught. Black snakes, rattlesnakes, and copperheads all live in the same kinds of places—woodsy and rocky country.

Fox snakes are also members of the *Elaphe* group. They do not climb as much as the other rat snakes and are usually found on the ground in the woods and brushy fields. Any snake of the *Elaphe* group needs a tall cage with a branchy tree or shrub to climb on. They sit coiled up on a high place and sun themselves. In the pilot black snake cage a pile of rocks makes a good sunning area. Be sure to keep the cage in a location where the snake can get out of the sun—or have a cave into which it can go to cool off.

Two more constrictors that make good pets are the famous boa constrictor from Central and South America and the reticulated python from Malaysia, Burma, and Vietnam. These two species belong to the giant snakes of the world. The boa constrictor does not grow much over eleven or twelve feet long, but the reticulated python can become over thirty feet long. Of course, the chance that either of these snakes will reach that size in your cages is slim. They could, though, grow so big that you would have trouble feeding them enough to keep them healthy.

If this happens, you should try to dispose of the snake to someone better able to care for it and get a smaller specimen for yourself. If the snake is a good specimen, healthy and contented with captivity, you might give it as an outright gift donation to your local zoo. Or you could sell it to an animal farm that has a display of exotic animals for public view. While both the boa constrictor and the python can

Boa Constrictor. *Constrictor constrictor.* When young, these are among the most colorful of snakes. Chocolate-brown, white and gray markings are vivid.

climb, it is not necessary to keep a real arboreal habitat for them. A good strong branch will serve well, and the boa constrictor especially will stretch out along it.

South American boa constrictors become quite tame. The Central American ones are a little more timid and sometimes try to bite. When the pythons are first caught they are quite wild and will strike and bite every chance they get. Both the boa constrictor and the python can give you a good bite, since they have big mouths that open very wide. They also have long sharp teeth and can hold on when they catch your finger. However, the bites are not very painful, are generally clean, and do not become infected. Treat them with antiseptic and a Band-aid.

Both the boa constrictor and the python need large water dishes to curl up in. They like to lie in the water after eating, and may stay there for several days digesting their food.

Sometimes a python will not feed when it is first caged. Weeks may go by before it will take anything to eat. You should put a mouse or small rat in the cage for fifteen or twenty minutes. If the snake does not show interest within that time, you should remove the food. Try again the next day. You may have to keep this up for several weeks, until finally the snake eats the animal.

When your pet starts to feed, there may be danger of overfeeding it. It may take as many mice or rats as you will offer it. If this happens, the chances are that it will become sick and throw them up. It is best to give your snake one little animal a day for two or three days, then one every other day for another two or three days. After that, you can put the snake on a regular feeding schedule. One good-sized rat or a couple of mice once a week should be plenty until the snake reaches six to seven feet. You then might have to increase the food by giving larger animals, such as small rabbits or guinea pigs, or feed it twice the amount of rats or mice.

A python in good health is one of the most beautiful snakes in the world. Its colored skin has all the hues of a rainbow. These colors keep moving as the snake moves. It looks like a beautiful gemstone. But this color is lost when the snake is sick or dead. Many snakes show a play of color, generally on the belly scales, but none as deep, bright and beautiful as

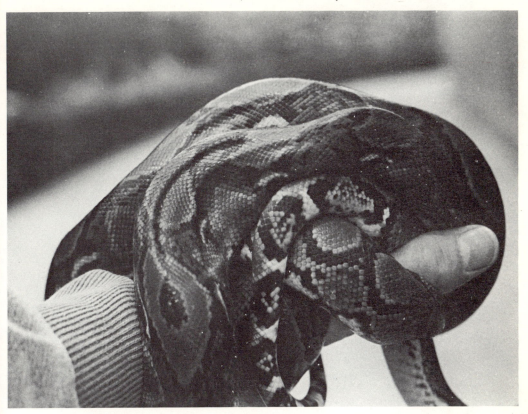

Reticulated Python. *Python reticulatus.* Notice the tight knot wrapped around the hand. Never handle a large constrictor alone, but always have someone standing by to help unwind it if it wraps around your neck.

the python. The only other snake I know with such color is a boa that comes from Central America. The colors are so strong and beautiful that the snake is called the rainbow boa. Rainbow boas make good pets, too. They are very tame.

Probably the tamest snake you can find is the indigo snake, which grows to a length of nine feet. It is about the only snake that seems to like to be handled. It will lie for long periods of time while you stroke its belly or its back. Indigo snakes have been known to follow their owners around like a puppy or kitten. They will feed readily and take food out of your hands. They are shiny blue-black everywhere except the throat, which is dark red. There is a play of rainbow color all over their skin. Indigo snakes are the ones used in circuses by snake dancers and snake "charmers" because they are so tame and like to be played with. They are not constrictors and do not squeeze their prey but swallow it alive. They will feed on rats, mice, birds, toads, frogs, and other snakes.

Indigo Snake. *Drymarchon corais couperi.* One of the easiest snakes to keep as a pet. They become very tame and often follow their keeper around the room.

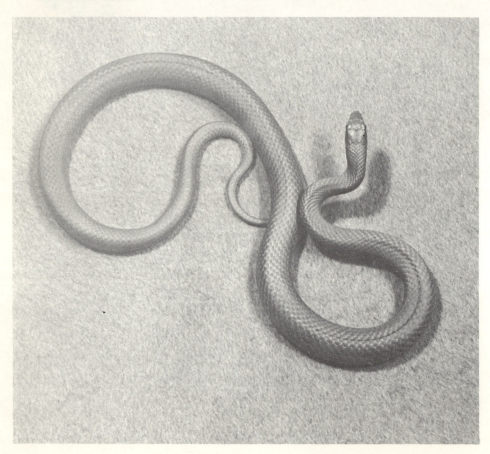

The indigo snake is sometimes called the gopher snake. This is because it hides in gopher tortoise burrows when it is being pursued. It will hide in other holes and burrows, of course, or in among rock piles. It is found in the southeastern United States, and is the largest snake in that part of the country.

Garter snakes are to be found everywhere in the country. They belong to the genus *Thamnophis*. While garter snakes can be kept in captivity, they do not make very good pets because they are generally fearful, and often bite. They have

California Red-sided Garter Snake. *Thamnophis s. parietalis.* This is one of the garter snakes that bite if they can get the chance. Of course, their bite is not dangerous, but it will make your finger bleed.

a very bad habit of releasing a foul smell when they are handled. This is caused by the snake emptying its anus or cloaca. Some individual specimens stop doing this after a while. Others never stop. Some garter snakes never become tame enough to handle without biting or trying to escape. Others calm down after a while and seem to accept captivity. It is difficult to say which specimen will do what. I have had a pair of Marcy's garter snakes that seemed perfectly contented in captivity. They had thirteen babies! The young of this species are born alive, instead of hatching from eggs.

Sometimes a garter snake will refuse to eat. If this happens, there is nothing much you can do except to get rid of it. Free it where you found it. You might try to give it to your zoo, except that the zoo will probably not want it either. Zoos are given so many snakes that they have no way of taking care of them all. If the specimen was a rare one or extra large, the zoo might be happy to have it, but for the small common garter snakes there is no room.

Garter snakes need something in their cages to hide under. A small piece of log, a pile of stones, even a flat piece of tree bark is good. They feed on insects, small frogs, worms, lizards, other snakes, and some good feeders will even take strips of raw lean beef. Many species of *Thamnophis* will eat fish, too. The little ribbon snake is a garter snake but does not seem to have the bad habits of smelling up itself or remaining wild. Ribbon snakes will eat fish readily, and they live well in captivity. While some of them may remain wild and fearful, most of them will become tame enough to handle without trouble.

One of the most unusual snakes you can find is the hognosed snake. This poor animal is the cause of more stupid and superstitious stories than almost any other living creature.

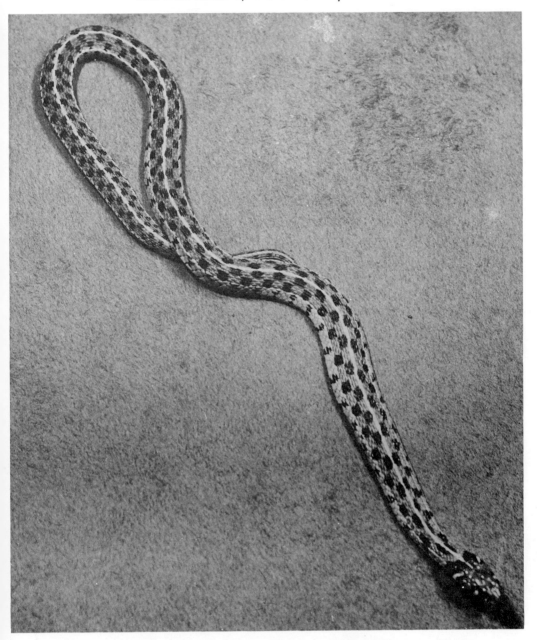

Marcy's Garter Snake. *Thamnophis marcianus.* One of the most beautifully marked of the garter snakes—tames very easily.

The hog-nosed snake has many local names, each of them pointing to something supposedly frightful about the reptile. It is called the spreading adder, puff adder, blowing adder, hissing viper, flat-headed adder, and others. All the names have either "adder" or "viper" in them. Adders and vipers are some of the deadliest snakes in the world. The hog-nosed snake is not deadly. It is not even poisonous. In fact, it is impossible to make a hog-nosed snake bite you. You can even push your finger into its mouth and still it will not bite. These snakes live in sandy places, and they like to burrow with their up-turned noses. They rarely eat anything but toads, although some have been known to eat frogs.

The hog-nosed snake has a bag of tricks that it uses when it is frightened or attacked by an enemy. This snake can spread a hood like a cobra. It flattens its head and raises it with the hood spread wide, so it looks exactly like a dangerous cobra! While it does this, it hisses very loudly. Usually this is enough for people who do not know about snakes.

If the cobra act does not frighten away the enemy, the hog-nosed snake will coil up with its tail raised in the center of the coil and stretch its neck out in an "S" curve like a rattlesnake. The tail is vibrated very rapidly, but it doesn't make any noise. The snake will strike just like a rattlesnake, but if you watch it closely, you will see that it doesn't even open its mouth!

As a last resort, the snake will go into convulsions, lash its body violently about, and roll its tongue in the dirt. Then it will roll over on its back and go limp. It is now "dead." If you go off a little distance and remain quiet, slowly the snake will roll over onto its belly and start to crawl away. Turn back to it and it will immediately flop onto its back, out will come the tongue, and you have a "dead" snake again.

But in a very short time the hog-nosed snakes can become

Heterodon contortrix in typical resting attitude. This snake is called the Hog-Nosed Viper, Spreading Adder, Hissing Viper and other names.

tame. They are short fat snakes with rough scales and dull brown, gray, or black coloring with mottles showing under the dark ground color. The tail is short and stubby. They do not move very fast, and are easy to catch.

A small brown snake called DeKay's snake is to be found all over the United States. These have even been found in Central Park, in the heart of New York City! The snake does not grow much longer than eight or ten inches, and is a pale brown color with darker brown markings on the back and sides. It feeds on grubs and earthworms. It is a shy feeder, and often, if it is swallowing a worm and you approach its cage, it will disgorge the food and refuse to eat for a long time afterward. This disgorging of food is a defense mechanism. If a snake has just fed, it has a full belly and is sluggish. On being attacked it would be less able to make a fast retreat. So if it disgorges its food it is much less sluggish and can flee rapidly.

Small brown snakes called Sonoras, similar to DeKay's snake, are found in this country also. They do not live in captivity as well as DeKay's snake, but some of them become tame and feed well. Look for these small brown snakes under stones or any other protection such as bark, old boards, or even large leaves. Usually they will coil up when you lift the stone from over them, and you can grab them quickly with your hand. They are easy to keep in small cages and you can keep several together without having trouble between them.

In recent years importers have been bringing several species of exotic snakes into this country to be sold in pet stores. One very interesting snake is the egg-eating snake from Africa. It is a fairly small snake, two to three feet long, with rough scales and a light brown body with darker blotches, and it only eats eggs. Since it feeds at night, you will have to watch in very dim light to see this process. It is remarkable to see an egg-eating snake swallow a hen's egg. The food is many times as big around as the snake's head, yet the animal can stretch its mouth over the egg until it is so swollen that you think it would burst. After the egg is down a way into the throat, the snake cuts through the shell with teeth that are located in its throat and the inside of the egg runs down its throat. Then the snake spits out the shell.

Another curious snake being imported is the Thailand water snake, or tentacled water snake. This snake has two short tentacles on the end of its nose and a short *prehensile* tail. It can wrap its tail around your finger and support itself in the air. In the wild, it wraps its tail around weeds or grasses growing in the river beds in Thailand, and remains quiet, waiting for food to swim by. It feeds on fish, crawfish, and other water life.

A strange thing about this snake is that when it is taken from the water it stiffens its body until it is rigid. The native name for the snake means "board snake" and it is almost as stiff as a board when it is handled. This snake must be kept in an aquarium of water, with some water plants growing in sand on the bottom. It is fed by dropping live fish into the water. The snake moves fast enough when it is after food, but it practically never moves at other times.

Water snakes can be found almost everywhere in this country. Many naturalists think that they are not very good pets. Usually water snakes do not feed well. They do not get very tame.

Yet my younger son had a water snake that became completely tame after a couple of weeks. He would wear the snake wrapped around his wrist like a bracelet, while riding his bicycle on his paper route. He wore the snake to school and it remained quiet all day. It fed from his hands. One

Thailand Water Snake. *Erpeton tentaculatum.* This odd creature will support itself for long periods of time by its strong, prehensile tail, actually tying a knot around the support.

day while he was showing it to boys at school the snake was frightened by one of the boys and crawled down the sink drain. The next day the superintendent found it and returned it to William, who had posted a reward notice on the bulletin board. While I do not recommend water snakes as pets, I must admit that there are exceptions.

Water snakes are not very pretty. They are dull dark brown, with very rough scales, and they have ugly heads. They look as though they should be poisonous, but they are not. They do have a good set of teeth, which can give you a real bite. They feed on fish, frogs, and tadpoles. Their cage should have water deep enough to swim and feed in, and a place for the snake to crawl out of the water.

Common Water Snake. *Natrix taxispilota.* Some water snakes will become tame and feed, but most of them remain nervous, fearful and do not eat in cages.

In the southeastern states there is the red-bellied snake, also called the mud snake, the hoop snake, the horn snake, and the stinging snake. On the end of its tail is a short sharp spine. If you were handling the snake and it was whipping around, this spine might scratch you, but it would be accidental. However, the spiny tail has given rise to a strange (untrue) story that the snake takes its tail in its mouth and rolls after you like a hoop. When it catches you, it lashes you with its tail. The snake very rarely tries to bite, and even then it would not hurt you.

Eastern Ring-necked Snake. *Diadophis punctatus.* The top is steel gray and the belly pale yellow, with tiny black spots along the sides.

The back of the snake is a beautiful glossy black and it has a deep brick-red color on the belly. Bars of red come up the sides, too. Red-bellied snakes are hard to keep in captivity. Young ones will sometimes feed, but older specimens rarely eat in captivity.

However, Dean Davis, the young naturalist to whom this book is dedicated, has a red-bellied snake that eats frogs with great relish. This is the first time I have ever seen one of these snakes eat. It is fairly young, not more than three feet long, and this species grows to six feet or more. Of course, it may stop feeding when it gets bigger.

There are many, many kinds of snakes other than the few I have mentioned here. Some of them might do well in cages, but many of our common snakes are not good pets. Ring-necked snakes are hard to get to feed. The smooth and the rough green snakes are the same. They are pretty, small,

California Striped Whipsnake, *Coluber lateralis*. These are one of the fastest of snakes. They are excellent tree climbers, too.

and slender. They like to climb trees and shrubs, but they refuse to feed in cages. Some of the boas will live and feed well in captivity. The rubber boa from the west coast of the United States is very tame and gentle.

The thing to do when you get a new species is to watch it closely for a time. Look it up in one of the snake books to make sure you know what kind it is. Then try to find out what kind of place it likes to live in. You can then make its cage as comfortable as possible for it. Watch when you put food in the cage to see if the snake is interested. If it takes food within a few days of its capture, the chances are that it will feed regularly. If it refuses food for weeks, then the best thing to do is to liberate it and try another kind. It is cruel to keep a snake that will not eat. It will only die.

CHAPTER 10

The Best Kinds of Turtles
to Keep as Pets

In one way, turtles are easier than snakes to keep as pets. This is because turtles cannot escape so easily. They cannot ooze through small holes. They cannot climb very well. Turtles live a long time, too—some live for more than twenty-five years in the house. You could find a nice turtle, tame it and set up a nice place for it to live in, and then grow up with your pet.

There are turtles that live only in water. Others always live on land. Then there are several kinds that live on land but go into the water, too. Some turtles can eat only under water. They cannot swallow their food in the air. There are several kinds of turtles that make good pets. They become tame easily and quickly.

Turtles sun themselves on rocks overhanging water, into which they can drop when an enemy approaches. You can put your turtle aquarium in or near a window where it will get some sun each day. Be sure, though, that there is a place for the turtles to get into the shade. Sun is good for all reptiles, but if they are trapped in the sun it will kill them. Reptiles are cold-blooded and their blood will heat up if they remain in the sun too long. A temperature will be reached that the animal cannot stand.

Remember that turtles carry the disease salmonella. This does not mean that you should never go near a turtle for the rest of your life. It does mean though, that you should exercise some health measures when handling your pet. First, *always* wash your hands after playing with your turtle or handling it in any way. *Never* hold the turtle up to your face, kiss it, or allow it to breathe into your face. It may sound silly for me to tell you not to kiss a turtle. It isn't very silly, though. Many people love their pets so much that they regularly hug and kiss them. It is a bad habit to kiss any animal. There is always the possibility of catching a disease from it. And, obviously, you should never put your turtle in any container that is used for food or for cooking.

If you practice these simple precautions, there should be very little danger of contracting any sickness or disease from your pets.

There are literally hundreds of different kinds of turtles. I am not even going to try to list them all here. It is not necessary. Most of them you will never even get to see outside of a zoo. Perhaps the best kinds of turtles for you to keep are those that live in the same kind of climate as you do. This means that most of the turtles will be those you can see in the streams, ponds, and rivers where you live.

Ordinary pond turtles make good pets because they will become quite tame, generally feed well, and live a long time in a cage if properly taken care of. Young specimens should be taken, rather than the old mossbacks. When pond turtles are old, moss, algae, and sometimes other water life grow on the shell. This is particularly true of the snapping turtles. Sometimes their shells are so covered with moss and mud that you cannot tell they are turtles at all! They lie on the bottom of the pond and remain very still. Their prey does not know that the mound of mud and moss is an enemy, either, until suddenly it is snapped up.

Perhaps the easiest kind of turtle to obtain is a young slider. They are now sold in such quantities that the dealers are no longer able to find enough wild ones to stock for their customers. For this reason, people have started to breed the common slider turtle. Georgia is the leading state for this industry. Thousands and thousands of young sliders are hatched each year on very large turtle-breeding farms.

The shells are bright green and yellow, and they are really very pretty little animals. The whole turtle becomes grayish when it is old. Male sliders or red-ears have longer claws on their feet than the females. They also have darker shells. Red-ears should be kept in an aquarium or container with a few inches of water and a dry place where they can climb up to sun themselves. The container should be kept in a warm place where it will get some sunshine each day. Be very careful to have a place shaded from the direct sunlight, though, or the animal may become overheated and die. From 75 to 85 degrees is the best temperature range for young turtles of this species. The temperature can drop a bit at night, but should not be allowed to go much below 60 degrees if at all possible.

Young red-ears like to eat in the water. They take food on dry land, but they prefer to feed submerged in the water. They should be fed small bits of *lean* beef, beef heart, small earthworms, meal-worms, and small pieces of raw chicken. Do not feed them cooked meat or smoked or pickled meat.

Vegetables should also be given them. A lettuce leaf, small pieces of raw carrot, a freshly shelled pea or two are acceptable. Small pieces of fruit are also good.

Don't forget that the food given young turtles should be

Red-eared Terrapin. *Pseudemys scripta*. This is the common little baby turtle sold by the thousands in pet shops, which die by the thousands because of improper food and care.

chopped into pieces that the little animals can swallow whole with no trouble. Turtles do not chew their food. They tear off chunks from larger pieces and swallow them, but it is much better to chop their food into sizes that they can manage without any trouble. If you plop a large hunk of meat into the turtle cage, it may foul the water before the turtle has eaten enough.

Always change the water as soon as it is no longer clear, clean, and sparkling. This means that you should feed your pets only as much as they will eat, and not so much that a lot of food remains in the water after feeding time. If you feed them one or two bits of meat and watch them eat it, then give them one or two more, you will soon learn about how much your animal will eat at one meal.

Chopped liver is good for turtles and they seem to like it. If your mother cooks fish, the raw entrails, chopped small, are very good for your pets. They contain vitamins needed for the turtles' health which are not found in other foods. A snail, with the shell crushed so the turtle can get at the meat, is also good food. Look for land snails under stones and logs in among the damp leaves of the woods and fields. Pieces of raw fish and small live fish are excellent foods. For live fish, you could use guppies. The minnows sold for fishing bait are too large for the young turtles. They are fine for grown specimens, though. Small tadpoles are eagerly eaten by young turtles.

Some other kinds of turtles found in pet stores, often in the same tank as the red-ears, are young map turtles, young snappers, and a pretty brown turtle with ridges down the center of its back called a sawback.

Sawbacks come from the southern part of the country, along the Mississippi Valley. They need warmer cage temperatures than do the red-ears or the map turtles. The same kinds of foods are good for all the turtles mentioned so far.

There are three main species of painted turtles—the Eastern, the Western, and the Southern. The Southern painted turtle has a bright yellow or white stripe down the middle of its back when it is young. When the animal is older, this stripe becomes red. The Eastern and Western painted turtles are very similar in appearance. The *plastron* (the bottom or belly part of a turtle's shell) of the Eastern painted turtle is orange, and has no markings of any kind on it. In the Western species, the plastron is covered with a fancy pattern. The *carapaces* or top shells of both the Eastern and the Western

Southern Painted Turtle. *Chrysemys picta dorsalis.* The Southern turtle differs from the Eastern painted turtle by having one yellow stripe down the middle of the back.

painted turtles look very much alike. If you have one that you cannot identify, merely turn it over and look at the plastron. If it is marked, your pet is Western. If it is plain, your turtle comes from the eastern part of the United States. The stripe down the back is enough identification for you to recognize the Southern painted turtle. The front claws of male painted turtles are very much longer than their rear claws. Sometimes the front ones are two or three times longer than the back ones. The males have long tails. Females of the painted turtles have shorter tails, and their claws are all nearly the same length.

Painted Turtle. *Chrysemys picta*. The plastron of painted turtle is plain yellow, and has no markings on it.

Painted Turtle. *Chrysemys picta.* This one is very common in the eastern part of the United States. It makes a good pet.

Bangkok Pond Turtle. *Malayemys subtrijuga.* Although this turtle comes from Asia, it must be kept cooler than most turtles. It eats snails.

Sometimes a pet store will import foreign turtles. Lately, many animals from the Far East have been brought into this country for sale. Among them are several different kinds of turtles. Some of them are not very easy to keep as pets. One pond turtle from Thailand is a good pet, though. This is the Siamese pond turtle, or Bangkok turtle. It comes from Thailand and Pakistan, and feeds on snails. In fact it is hard to get it to eat anything else, although it will sometimes eat lean beef or liver. Its shell is dark brown with a yellow border, and has three high ridges along the carapace. The temperature of its home must be cooler than the homes of other turtles—from 60 to 70 degrees.

Snapping turtles are not too good as pets because they are always nasty and when they get a little old, they try to bite. The very young ones are gentler, and, even if they do try to bite, they cannot hurt you very much. An older snapper can really injure you. Also, snappers grow very large and you would have to have an enormous place to keep them in if you had them for a long time.

Spotted turtles are often seen crossing roads. They are similar to the painted turtles, and they, too, make good pets. They will eat meat, fish, vegetables, and some fruits, and like to feed in the water. They become very tame and are very gentle. The males have longer tails than the females, and brown eyes. The females have orange eyes and a yellow stripe on the lower jaw. The male lacks this stripe.

Spotted turtles must have water enough to swim around in, and a flat rock or log where they can climb out to bask in the sun. When you come near, they quickly slide off the rock into the water, swimming around underneath the rock or log to hide. For this reason they are very difficult to catch in the wild, unless you find one traveling from pond to pond, which they often do, crossing the roads along the way.

Another aquatic or water turtle that lives well in captivity is the musk turtle. When you first catch one, it gives off a very bad odor. But after the turtle has been in captivity awhile and becomes tame, it does not release its smell. However, if a strange person picks it up suddenly, or frightens the animal in any way, it will still smell.

Most of the musk turtles I have found have a thick coating of algae or moss on the shells. This is difficult to remove, although you can scrape it off carefully and slowly, so as not to frighten the animal. Musk turtles are called stinkpots, and this name fits them very well. These interesting turtles are among the few that can actually climb small trees. It is very odd to look up into a tree and see a turtle sitting on a branch.

Mud turtles also give off a bad odor. The yellow mud turtle is a smooth, trim, and pretty animal, and becomes tame after a short time in a cage. Male musk turtles and male mud turtles both have thicker, heavier tails than the females. They also have a hard tip on the tail that the females do not have. Males have two heavy rough scales on each hind foot. Females do not. Both these species are water turtles and need water deep enough to swim around in, and big enough in area to afford them a good pool. It would be difficult to keep them in an outdoor pool because they can climb. Of course, if you could cover their pool with an escapeproof screen of some kind, you could easily keep them outdoors. Float a piece of wood in their water or have a flat rock sticking out so they can climb up out of the water if they like.

The musk and mud turtles eat meat, fish, and some water plants. If you go to a tropical fish store, you can get bunches of anacharis, cabomba, and other water plants that are used in fish aquariums. These are very good for turtles, too, and you can plant them in gravel in the bottom of the water in your turtle tank. The animals will enjoy nibbling on them when they are hungry.

Snapping Turtle. *Chelydra serpentina.* The shells of these turtles are almost always covered with moss and algae, giving them a muddy, dirty appearance.

Musk Turtle. *Sternothaerus odoratus.* When newly captured, these turtles give off a very bad smell. After they become tame, however, they stop smelling up their cages.

Yellow Mud Turtle. *Kinosternon flavescens flavescens.* This one has a bad stink, too, when it is first captured.

A turtle pond you can set up.

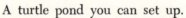

Often turtles eat meat and insects when they are very young. These form their main diet at that time. Slowly, however, they will eat more and more leafy vegetables, fruits and berries, until, when they are fully grown, they are almost entirely vegetarian.

Land turtles may be a bit easier to keep than water or semi-aquatic ones. The prettiest of the land turtles, I think, is the wood turtle. While I class this turtle as a land turtle, it is really a semi-aquatic species. However, it lives so well on land and lives so long in the house, that you really do not have to give it a semi-aquatic home for it to be contented and healthy. This one has a dark brown shell that is beautifully marked in a regular pattern of designs. The plastron has dark patches of color around the edges. The center is

Wood Turtle. *Clemmys insculpta.* The carapace of wood turtles is very beautifully sculptured with shell-like markings.

Wood Turtle. *Clemmys insculpta*. The plastron of this animal has broad blotches of dark chestnut on each plate.

plain. Male wood turtles have much stronger and more curved front claws than the females. The plastron of a male wood turtle is slightly hollow. The plastron of a female is slightly rounded out.

Wood turtles make wonderful pets. They live a long time and become very tame. They eat almost anything that you eat—raw fruits, vegetables, lean beef, fish, chicken. They should also have some muscle meat like chicken or beef heart. Liver is good for them, too. Once a week or so you could put a drop of cod-liver oil on the bits of meat you feed to your wood turtle. In fact, this would be excellent for any of your turtle pets.

Another land turtle is the box turtle. There are several species of box turtles in this country. The common box

Eastern Box Turtle. *Terrapene carolina carolina.* These gentle creatures will live for years, and, if put out in your garden often will not wander away, but remain near its constant source of food. When discovered in the woods they are nearly invisible due to the markings on the carapace.

turtle is found in the eastern part of the United States. Blanding's turtle is found in the northeastern part of the country. The three-toed box turtle comes from the southeastern part of the United States and around the Gulf of Mexico. The ornate box turtle is the one found in the central and western part of the country. There are a few other species of box turtles, but some of them are just subspecies.

Most box turtles like the same kind of habitat. A woods aquarium should be set up for them. They like dead leaves, a small log, and a few rocks. The leaves can be kept slightly damp but not wet. You can have some dirt on the bottom of the tank, and a dish of water that is large enough and deep enough for your pet to get into. Some box turtles like to eat with their heads under water.

Male box turtles generally have lower carapaces than the

Three-toed Box Turtle. *Terrapene c. triunguis.* They make good pets. They live for many years and eat well in captivity.

females. There is a fairly deep hollow at the rear of the plastron of the males. The eyes of the males are brightly colored pink or red. The eyes of the females are darker and sometimes are gray or brown or very dark red.

If you keep your box turtles outdoors, you must give them a place in which they can dig down into the dirt when they hibernate during the winter. If possible, they should have not less than eighteen inches of dirt to dig into. If there is less than this, after they have dug down for the winter, you can pile hay on top of their burrow to help keep them from freezing.

I might mention here, before closing the chapter on turtles, that a very favorite food of box turtles, and other land turtles, too, is raw mushrooms.

CHAPTER 11

The Best Kinds of Lizards to Keep as Pets

There are so many different kinds of lizards in the world that I could write a book or two on them alone. Many lizards make good pets, yet some cannot be kept in captivity. They will not live. Some of them grow so big that it would be very difficult to keep them in a cage in the house. Of all the reptiles, I believe the most brilliant and beautifully colored ones are found among the lizards. They have metallic colors: blue, green, gold, red—all the colors of the rainbow. There are several that make good pets, and that you can obtain easily, either by catching them yourself or buying them in pet stores.

The most common lizard found in pet stores is the little green anole, which is often called a chameleon. The true chameleon is a very strange animal, and not very often found for sale.

The only way an anole can drink is by licking drops of dew off the leaves of plants. In their natural habitat, the animals drink in the early morning or the late evening, when the dew forms on the grasses and plants. In captivity the only way they can get their water is by having a plant grow-

American "chameleon." *Anolis carolinensis*. These little lizards will get to be tame if you handle them often and feed them properly. You can wear them on your shirt after they get to know you.

ing in their cage and having water sprinkled on the leaves of the plant two or three times each day. It is an easy matter to put a small potted philodendron in the cage for your anole, and to sprinkle it in the morning and evening.

Anoles eat small meal-worms, flies, fruit flies, spiders, small grasshoppers, and many kinds of insects. Their cage should be kept warm. The ideal temperature is between 80 and 85 degrees. The temperature can drop a little at night but remember that the nights where these animals come from are quite warm. The atmosphere should be kept humid in their cage. The easiest way to do this is to cover the bottom of the cage with coarse aquarium gravel that has been washed until the water runs clear. Then, when you put the gravel in the cage, wet it with a cup of water. As the gravel dries out, you can add a little water. You do not want to have the water standing in the bottom of the cage, just damp gravel.

In most parts of this country, swifts are very common. These are called by a lot of different names in different areas. Fence lizards, fence swifts, rail lizards, blue-bellied swifts are a few of the names given to these interesting animals. They have rough scales and the bellies of the males have two dark blue patches on the sides. As their name implies, they are swift. It is almost impossible to get close enough to catch them. As soon as they see you they jump away.

About the easiest way to catch them is with a long slender pole and a noose made of heavy sewing thread. Remember that a fence lizard will bite when it is first caught, so do not be so surprised that you let it go when it nips your finger. The bite is nothing. It rarely even breaks the skin. Actually it is a little pinch rather than a real bite. After a fence lizard has been kept for a while, it will become

Blue-bellied Swift. *Sceloporus undulatus*. These are one of the fastest of the lizards. They like to sun themselves on rails of fences and low branches.

tame enough for you to handle and play with. Remember its name, though. It is a swift! At any time, unless you have a secure hold on it, it can dart away so fast that it is gone before you know it. It can easily run up a wall, up a tree or anything at all.

Blue-bellied swifts eat all kinds of insects. They love moths and butterflies, and will eat meal-worms, grasshoppers, crickets, different kinds of beetles, and many other insects. They can drink water out of a water dish, lapping it with their tongues. Some dirt and leaves should be on the bottom of the cage, with a rock or two to hide under, and a log to sit on in the sun. They love to stretch out on a fence rail and sun themselves. The temperature should be warm in the daytime.

Wall Lizard. *Lacerta muralis*. These are fast, beautiful and very nervous animals. They live well in captivity, but it is difficult to hold them.

About 80 is fine; although they will be comfortable at 75 degrees, it should not be much less than that except at night.

Pet stores often sell lizards from other countries. One of these is from Europe, and it lives in the same kind of climate as we have. It is called the wall lizard and is very beautiful. It has a bright green body, dark blue patches along the sides and back, and suggestions of other colors. It needs about the same kind of cage and temperature as the fence lizards, and will eat the same foods. The European wall lizards will live well and a long time, but they are nervous and do not like to be handled very much. They try to escape if you take them from the cage. The best way to hold a lizard is to let its body lie in your hand, and catch

Basilisk. *Basiliscus americanus.* These lizards can run across the surface of water for short distances.

a hind leg between your thumb and forefinger, holding it firmly, but not so tightly as to hurt the animal's foot. It may pull a few times, trying to get loose, then it will usually lie quietly after the attempt to pull free.

Another imported lizard that can be bought in pet stores is the common basilisk. This is one of the larger lizards. It reaches a length of two feet or more. Basilisks are truly odd-looking members of the great family of lizards. Dark brown in color, they have wide flapping ridges running down their backs and tails. They live along riverbanks in Central America, and can run so fast that they often run right out across the surface of water.

Basilisks eat large insects, smaller lizards, small mammals like mice, frogs, fish, and other prey. They like temperatures around 80 degrees. They will live in a dry cage, but like to have enough water to soak in at times. They do need a large cage, though, because they are large lizards. Basilisks have very large mouths and their bite can be painful.

In the western and southwestern parts of this country there is a very good-looking reptile called the alligator lizard. This lizard is reddish brown, and its skin is like the skin of an alligator. There are black and white markings down the back and sides. Its diet consists of meal-worms and almost all other insects, and it will also eat small lizards of other species. The cage for the alligator lizard should have some sand and leaves in the bottom, and a log or a couple of rocks to climb up on. The cage should be very warm with a lot of sun, but there must be some shady place where the lizard can go to cool off if he gets too hot. The alligator lizard drinks out of a water dish.

Also from the South and West in the desert country come the little fat roly-poly lizards that are incorrectly called "horned toads." These animals are not toads but true lizards. They must be kept hot in order to live and remain healthy. They do well at temperatures between 80 and 90 degrees. They are "dewdrop drinkers," which means that you should have a plant or a few leaves to sprinkle water on for them to drink. They will sometimes lap at a water dish, but they must have sprinkled water to do really well.

Their favorite food is ants, and they will eat hundreds of ants at a meal. In the summer, you can take them outside in a portable cage without a bottom, and put them over an anthill. If it is warm enough, your pet will sit at the opening of the anthill gobbling up the ants as fast as they come out of the ground. You must be certain, though, that the cage is secure and tight all around the bottom, or the pet will crawl out and escape. They can get out of a very narrow space, because their bodies are so flat.

Southern Alligator Lizard. *Gerrhonotus multicarinatus.* It is said that this lizard, when attacked by a predator, takes a hind foot in its mouth to make an endless ring to avoid being swallowed. I have never seen this take place.

Crowned Lizard or Coast "Horned Toad." *Phrynosoma coronatum.* The camouflage coloration of this animal is remarkable. It is almost invisible when you are looking right at it.

"Horned toads" are very fearful-looking beasts. They are covered with rough warts and have rows of spines around their necks. They look as though they are ferocious and could be very dangerous. Actually they are among the gentlest of all animals. They never, never bite. Usually they are very slow and sluggish when they move about, but they can run very fast at times, so be careful when playing with them outside their cage.

When horned lizards are frightened, they react in a very odd way. They squirt a few drops of blood out of the corners of their eyes. Nothing much is known about this defense action, but we think that the blood stings the eyes of its enemies.

The cages for these animals should have not less than three inches of sand in the bottom, a rock or two to climb on, and some kind of plant to sprinkle with water, as well as a small water dish. Besides ants, horned lizards will eat meal-worms, spiders, moths, crickets, and other insects.

The desert spiny lizard is closely related to the blue-bellied swift, and looks very much like a swift. The desert lizard is usually larger and fatter. It is also a very fast runner, and can run right up a wall. This reptile eats all kinds of insects and also smaller lizards. The desert lizard is nicely colored. Some of them have a black collar edged in white around their necks. Its cage should be hot and dry. It drinks dewdrops *and* from a dish.

From the desert, also, come the collared lizards. These are beautifully colored in bright green, bright blue, with a black and white collar around the neck. They do not live too well in captivity. One reason is that the cage is usually not kept warm enough. It must be hot! The best temperature is not less than 80 degrees and up to 90 or even 95 degrees. Since collared lizards are fast runners, they should have a

Desert Spiny Lizard. *Sceloporus magister*. If these escape your grasp, they are almost impossible to recapture, since they are very fast and can run right up a wall.

long cage in which they can run when they want to. When a collared lizard gets up speed, he runs on his hind feet with his body upright. Collared lizards, like most desert animals, drink dewdrops from plants and rocks in the early morning and at night. They eat all kinds of insects and, if you are not careful, your fingers as well. They are particularly fond of grasshoppers, katydids, locusts, and crickets.

A very interesting lizard, native to this country, is the "glass snake." It is really a legless lizard. It has eyelids and can close them, and has ears—two things that a snake does not have. The fact that it is quite large—"glass snakes" reach a length of almost four feet—and has no legs makes some people think it is a snake. Usually "glass snakes" are not good pets, because they frighten so easily that they cannot be handled at all.

144

"Glass Snake." *Ophisauris attenuatus.* The young female specimen I had ate out of our hands and was very tame.

"Glass Snake." They love the giant mites which look like daddy longlegs spiders.

Once in a while you will find one that is very tame. I had one that regularly fed out of our fingers! She was one of the daintiest animals we ever kept, and was the pet of the entire family. Our little pet never lashed about at all, but allowed us to handle her as much as we wanted. Usually one of these lizards will whip about when it is picked up and snap off its tail very easily. Often the tail will break into two or more sections, this being the reason for the name "glass snake." However, our little pet would lie curled up in our laps or in our hands and would eat all the food we offered her. She loved spiders and giant mites, the very long-legged animals that look like "daddy longlegs" spiders.

The "glass snakes" eat all kinds of insects, but seem to like spiders best of all. They also drink water out of a dish. They are burrowing animals, and should have three or four inches of clean, slightly damp earth in their cages. They do not climb, so a branch is not necessary, but a couple of rocks for them to bask on are appreciated.

It is easy to tell the females of these lizards, because the females have a long fold in the skin on the sides of the body. The reason for this fold is to allow the body to swell up when it becomes full of eggs. The female's skin would pop if it did not have enough slack in it to stretch when she was ready to lay her eggs—up to thirty or more at one time. When the time comes to lay, she scoops out a hollow in the ground, generally under a piece of bark or a stone, and lays all her eggs in the hollow. Then she curls up around the eggs as though she was setting on them. Actually she does not keep the eggs warm. If she is not fed enough while the eggs are hatching, she will eat her own eggs! You would do well, when you have a "glass snake" that lays eggs, to remove them from her cage and keep them in an incubator such as described in Chapter 14, "Breeding Reptiles."

Of course, you all are familiar with the baby "alligators" that are sold in most pet stores, but these are not alligators. They are Central American and South American caymans. True, they look something like an alligator, but that is because both alligators and caymans are crocodilians. The crocodile and another very odd creature called a gavial belong to this family. Crocodilians are kept in a separate group by most herpetologists, but since I am only going to describe the one, I have put him in with the lizards because he *looks* like a lizard.

Hundreds of thousands of young caymans are killed every year by improper diet and care. The pet store salesmen

Cayman. *Caiman sclerops.* These little fellows can give you a good nip, and will, every chance they get! Keep them very warm.

147

may not tell you what these animals need to survive, and unless you read it somewhere, you will not know either. Two things are important to keep caymans alive—heat and the proper food. Caymans must be kept very warm. Eighty-five degrees is fine for them and they can stand even higher temperatures—up to 90 degrees. The temperature should not drop much below 60 degrees at night.

Caymans need meat and lots of it, but they need whole meat. This means that strips of lean beef, for instance, are fine to feed them, but they will not thrive on such a diet. They need the muscle-fiber meat that is found in a whole animal. If you feed them pieces of beef heart, chicken heart, chicken gizzard, whole fish, and things like that they will live well and be healthy. Whole mice—alive—are wonderful food for them.

Crocodilians feed by shaking their prey until they tear it apart. The cage for your cayman should be large enough to allow it to swim about in the water and still have a place for it to climb out on. The water area should be big enough to allow the cayman to catch his mouse when you drop it into the water, then shake it from side to side in order to eat it. The mouse, after you drop it into the water, will start to swim, and, as soon as the cayman sees it, he will grab it right in the water. White mice are available from almost every pet store and ten-cent store, or you can raise some yourself. When the cayman is small, two mice each week should be plenty.

One thing to remember about caymans, and about all crocodilians, for that matter, is that they bite. When they bite you know you've been bitten. Remember the saying, "He has teeth like a crocodile"? There is a reason for that saying.

Very unusual are the armadillo lizards from Africa. They

are called armadillo lizards because of the way they protect themselves. They live around piled rocks so they can scoot in among them to hide, whenever an enemy approaches. If one is ever caught away from a safe refuge among the rocks, it will take the end of its tail in its mouth and curl up into a tight ball, just like an armadillo! The entire head, back, and tail of the armadillo lizard are covered with strong, very hard scales, and when one is rolled up like that, its soft belly is well protected, and its enemy cannot get through the hard armor scales of its back.

Armadillo Lizard. They have armored scales very much like the animal for which they are named. They do not smell good, though!

The only armadillo lizard I ever had was a borrowed specimen that I kept to study and to photograph. It had a very strong disagreeable smell. I do not know whether or not this smell is usual with this species, but if it is, I would certainly look around for another kind of pet. This one is the real skunk of the reptile family!

Armadillo lizards eat all kinds of insects, and drink from a water dish. They like warm dry cages and a lot of sun to bask in. They like a pile of rocks in their cage so they can hide and feel protected. They are very pretty to look at. They have a light chestnut color, and their rough scales are polished and attached in very regular rows. The tail scales are very spiny, and the end of the tail is blunt and ends in a sort of brush of scales.

Green lacertas are sometimes offered for sale in pet stores, and these are among the gentlest and most beautiful of the lizards. They are easily identified as to sex. The males are solid yellow-green, and the females, although they are the same color, have two whitish stripes bordered with black patches running down the back. These beautiful lizards come from Europe and can adapt to our climate quite well, although they should never be allowed to get very cold. They eat meal-worms, moths, grasshoppers, crickets, and many other kinds of insects and they drink water out of a dish.

The proper cage for lacertas should have clean dirt mixed with equal amounts of clean sand or aquarium gravel in the bottom—about three inches deep. Pieces of moss, a slab of bark, and a small log can be set on top of the soil. A few rocks should be piled to make a small hill with crevices between large enough for the lizards to crawl into and hide. The soil should be kept just slightly moist, but not wet. Dead leaves from the woods can be put on top of the dirt not covered by the moss, bark, log, and rocks. The pets will come out and bask in the sun on top of the log or rocks, going under the bark or rocks at night.

I had one pair of these wonderful lizards that mated in their cage. The female later laid five eggs, buried in the dirt under the bark and moss. They are very calm animals, and not at all hysterical as some of the lizards are. The best temperature for lacertas is about 75 to 85 degrees, and must not drop to less than 50 degrees at night.

Probably the easiest of all lizards to keep as pets are the beautiful common iguanas from Central and South America. These are easy to keep because they are strictly vegetarian. This means that they eat fruits, vegetables, and melons, all of which are available throughout the winter. Iguanas must be kept warm. They come from very humid, hot countries, where the daytime temperature often goes well above 100 degrees. From 80 to 90 degrees is fine for your pets. It can drop as low as 55 or 60 at night, provided you can warm them up in the morning. If it is cold in your house, then you should keep an electric light bulb in a reflector on top of the cage to supply them with warmth.

Iguanas drink from a water dish, but they love assorted plants in their cage. They nibble on a leaf or two during the day. They should be fed chopped vegetables such as lettuce, grated carrots, raw peas or raw string beans, and chopped bits of almost any fruit. They love pears, apples, peaches, cherries, bananas, and many more. Chopped raw spinach leaves are eaten readily. In the winter months when fresh fruit may be hard to find, canned fruit cocktail is acceptable. Drain it well before giving it to your pets, and chop the pieces smaller than they are in the can.

Until the iguanas are a year old, you should put a few drops of cod-liver oil on their lettuce leaves every other day, or at least twice a week. A few small meal-worms should

Common Iguana. *Iguana iguana*. These handsome animals live very well in captivity, and, indeed, make one of the very best reptile pets.

also be dropped in with their vegetable food. They will stop eating meal-worms after a time, but they seem to need some when they are young. Iguanas do not chew their food, but swallow it whole. This is why you should chop everything fine for them. If you put a few different kinds of plants in small pots in their cage, you will find them nibbling on one or more. As soon as you see which ones they prefer to eat, you can make sure that one of this kind of plant is always in the cage.

The pair of iguanas I have are very fond of pansy plants and begonia leaves. The begonia is the plain, common kind that is found in grocery stores for less than fifty cents. In the summer the pansy plants are no problem. We plant a border of them along our sidewalk, and every week or so dig up one, put it into a small flowerpot, and put it in the cage. Of course, the plants in the cage must be watered, or they will die.

Iguanas have very long tails—as long as the head and body together, sometimes even longer. They need a large cage to live in. Also, they must have something in the cage to climb up on, such as branches. Unless they can climb, they will not remain healthy, and will soon die. I keep our pair on the sun porch, and every morning we open their cage and let them free. They climb all around on the potted plants we keep on the porch, and they climb up the window drapes to hang on them in the sun. All day they follow the sun around the porch, and at night, after the sun goes down, they find a corner where they go to sleep until we put them back into their cage for the night.

At least once a day we pick them up and handle them. Having their bellies petted seems to be their greatest enjoyment. This daily handling keeps them very tame, and at feeding time they take food right out of our fingers with no fear at all. The food dish should be a large shallow one. Iguanas like to walk in their food dish when they feed.

Our iguanas are about eighteen inches long now. They are about two years old. These beautiful lizards get to be six feet long. Of course, long before they reach that size they will be too big to keep in a small cage in the house, and we will have to look around for a place to put them. As long as they are healthy and contented, there is a good chance that, when they are larger than usual for house pets, the zoo will take them.

The real aristocrat of the lizard family is the true Old World chameleon. There are many species of this animal. Chameleons have all kinds of unusual head shapes. Some

Jackson's Chameleon. *Chamaeleo jacksoni.* This grumpy-looking fellow looks like a prehistoric dinosaur. Very gentle and tame.

of them have a shield that runs back from the back of the head over the neck. Others have heads that are squared off with a hollow on the top like a basin. Still others have one horn on the top of the head, or two horns, or three, and one even has four horns!

African chameleons are not very often available in pet stores, but sometimes the larger stores carry them. Nothing is quite like these strange, strange creatures. They move so slowly that you want to reach in and give them a boost with your finger.

Their feet are like pairs of tongs. Of course, their feet are perfect for their way of life. Chameleons are completely *arboreal.* This means that they live only in trees and shrubs, and practically never live on the ground. They cannot walk too well on the ground, and have a very funny waddle when they try. It is a different story in the trees, however. There their tong feet grasp around slender twigs and branches, giving them a very secure hold.

Their tails are prehensile. They can grasp with their tails just as well as some monkeys. Often you will see one walk out of the very tip of a branch, then let go with both front feet and extend its body away out in the air. Behind it, it hangs on with its hind feet and a curl of its tail. Slowly it extends itself out—until you think it is going to fall down, but the tail just straightens out more and more to allow it to stretch. Suddenly POP! its tongue shoots out for a distance equal to the entire length of the body and snaps up a fly or other insect. The tongue moves so fast that you can barely see it.

The eyes of these marvelous animals are mounted in little turrets like the guns of fighter planes. Each eye can move independently of the other. The animal can look forward with the right eye and rearward with the left eye at the same time, or up with one eye and down with the other.

One great difficulty in keeping African chameleons is the fact that they must be kept hot—not less than 80 degrees and 90 degrees is better. At night the temperature can drop to 60 degrees or so. During the winter, feeding them is a big problem, since they feed only on living insects and do not like meal-worms very much. Once in a while a specimen will eat meal-worms, but not usually.

In the summer, feeding a chameleon is easier because you can take the pet outdoors and put it on a tree or shrub. Put it where you can watch it, because it can get away from you very easily if you are not watching closely. If it disappears among the branches you can look right at it without seeing it. When you take it out, tie a piece of raw meat to the branch. In fact, it would be a good idea to tie the meat on the branch an hour or so before you take your lizard outside. The meat will attract flies and other insects, and your pet will sit on the branch and pick them off one at a time with his tongue. Just like a kind of nature cafeteria.

Common Chameleon. *Chamaeleo chamaeleon.* A good way to feed your chameleon is to tie a piece of meat on a branch to draw flies, and let your pet catch his own dinner!

Chameleons are dewdrop drinkers. They *must* have lots of water, and the only way they can get it is by licking drops off plant leaves. Keep a wide-leafed plant in the cage and sprinkle the leaves with water until they drip, at least twice every day. Four times would be better and six times best.

The cage should be as high as possible to allow the biggest branch you can stuff into it for climbing places. Some chameleons are egg layers and others have their young alive. The egg-laying kind like deep dirt on the bottom of their cage. This is, of course, necessary only if you are going to try to breed them and raise some young ones. In any event, some dirt should be on the bottom to give the animal a sense of security.

There is no point in telling you which species are egg-layers and which are live-bearers, because I do not know what species you would be able to get. I can tell you, though, that the three-horned species called Jackson's chameleon have their young alive. My pair presented me with twenty-one little ones one morning, much to my surprise. The young are born in sacs and, a short time after birth, stretch their noses and tails out far enough to break the sac, after which they crawl out and set forth to find food. Fruit flies are the ideal food for young chameleons, and if you have any of these lizards, you should keep a few fly farms going just in case you get any young. Remember that the seasons are reversed with them. The young will be born in our fall, not our spring.

CHAPTER 12

The Best Kinds of Geckos to Keep as Pets

If lizards come in all colors, then geckos come in all shapes. Shapes of tails, rather—and feet! Geckos are wonderful little members of the reptile family. They run up the wall and across the ceiling as though they were on the plain flat floor. And they do this without sticky feet. A gecko's foot is covered with tiny ridges on the bottom of each toe. Each ridge is covered with even tinier short, stiff, hooked hairs. When it puts its foot down, the toes are curled *backward*. As the foot comes into contact with the surface the toes are rolled down flat. The tiny hooks grip every microscopic irregularity in the surface. Even glass is not so smooth that it does not present ridges for the gecko's toes to grip! When the gecko lifts its foot, first the toes must be curled back upward to disengage the tiny gripping hooks. No matter how fast a gecko runs, it must use this curling and uncurling action of its toes.

The feet of geckos come in many, many different shapes. The toes of some are paddle-shaped. Others are shaped like the ends of rowboat oars. Still others are long and thin. The tails of geckos are as varied as their toes. One species has a tail shaped like a leaf. Others have tails like fat bulbs.

Some have long, normal lizard-like tails. Usually the gecko eats more food than it needs during the active months and stores the excess fat in the tail, which grows enormously. Then, when food is hard to find during the off season, the animal rests most of the time, remaining so inactive that it does not use up much energy. The gecko lives off the fat in the tail just as the hibernating bear lives off the fat under his skin. By the end of the lean season, the gecko might have a skinny scrawny tail, but this soon regains its fat plump shape after the animal stores up the available food.

Most geckos are afraid much of the time they are in captivity. They do not like to be handled, and they try to bite when picked up. The majority of little geckos do no damage with their teeth. They practically never break the skin, and just give you a nip. Not the tokay geckos, though. They have teeth like a crocodile's, and use them!

Tokay geckos were so named because they are supposed to have a call that sounds like "to-kay." The specimen I have barks like a dog, and, if you were not looking at it when it barked, you would think it *was* a dog! After keeping this reptile for over a year, one afternoon when it was still in its winter rest cycle, and no one was in the room with it, we heard a loud call clear through the house. At first it was the usual bark, and we knew it was our tokay gecko. Then, very clearly and distinctly, it called, "To-kay! To-kay! To-kay!" Six times this word was repeated, and then we understood how it got its name.

During the summer he eats grasshoppers and katydids by himself, as long as they are large ones. The small ones he refuses to eat. The same with crickets. Very large specimens do not last very long in his cage, but the little fellows always stay around until they die and dry up.

Tokay Gecko. *Gekko gecko*. They are beautiful creatures, with many color phases, but they bite—hard!

In the fall and winter he eats only meal-worms. He will not eat them by himself, however. We have to feed them to him. The way we do that is to open his cage and wait until I have a good chance to grab him behind the head. When I have him pinned to the side of his cage, I work my fingers around his body until I can lift him out with my hold still around his neck, and his feet secure in the palm of my hand. Of course, his mouth is wide open and he squirms around trying to chop off my hand. While his mouth is open, I hold him and my wife starts to fill it up with meal-worms. He holds from twenty to twenty-four at a clip. When his mouth is full I slowly and gently squeeze his jaws shut, carry him to his cage, and put him down on the floor. Then I snatch my hand out of the cage just an inch ahead of his final snap! Unless you have fast reflexes, a brave helper, and good nerves, leave the tokay geckos alone. They are interesting, but they are just too much trouble to be fun.

The tokay gecko has interesting eyes. The eyeball is golden, and the pupil is wavy. When the iris closes, there are four pinhole openings left in the pupil. This allows the animal to see during the daytime, since tokay geckos are normally nocturnal. They will eat all kinds of insects. Some of them will feed themselves, however, the majority have to be fed as I described above. They like it about 75 to 90 degrees. They drink water from a dish and also lap dewdrops, so sprinkle a plant for them each day as well as providing a water dish. Tokay geckos come from Malaysia and are egg-laying animals.

Another imported gecko is the pretty little striped gecko from Pakistan. These are gentle animals and do not try to bite every time they are handled. A word of caution here about handling geckos. Some of them have the shocking habit of jumping right out of their skins when handled. They lash around, trying to escape your hand, then the skin splits and the raw animal plops onto the floor, leaving you holding its empty hide! Besides shocking you, it is generally fatal to the gecko, so beware.

The Pakistani striped gecko is gray with six light stripes down the back and sides. Between the stripes are rows of regular round dots of white edged in black. There are several wavy bands of white edged with black on the head. These geckos are small, about four inches long. They eat small insects and meal-worms. The cage should have sand in the bottom, a few small rocks for them to scamper around, and some sort of cave to hide in. They are dewdrop drinkers,

Pakistani Striped Gecko. Here is a tiny animal, scarcely more than 3″ long. It sings at night!

and they will at times lap water from a dish. Keep the cage about 75 to 85 degrees—a little lower at night.

Probably the gentlest and most beautiful of the geckos is another one from Pakistan. This is the leopard gecko, or the fat-tailed gecko. I have a pair of them and they mated and the female laid five eggs. Their skin is pink, covered with little bumps. There are dark spots over the entire skin. The eyes are beautiful—silver eyeballs, with vertical pupils, like a cat's. The eyelids are made of a row of pure white knobs. The leopard geckos like to be handled if you do not close them up in your hand. If you do so, they will fight to get free.

Leopard Gecko. *Eublephorus macularis.* One of the gentlest of geckos. Does not mind being handled, but dislikes to be confined in the hands. Hold it in your open hands instead.

If you just hold them in your open hand, they will allow you to stroke their bellies and backs, and seem to enjoy it. Our pair eats meal-worms almost exclusively. Only rarely will they take other insects. When they are in a stage of rest and near-hibernation, I put food into their cage every second day and watch to see if they eat any. When a couple of hours pass without the food being touched, I remove it until the next time. Water is always in the dish.

During this time of hibernation, we do not handle them very much. It would frighten them to be played with during the time they are normally inactive. We keep them at 80 degrees, letting the cage drop to about 60 at night. A light bulb is always burning in a reflector on the top of their cage. The cage has dirt in half the bottom area and sand in the

African House Gecko. *Hemidactylus* species. This little animal is covered with tiny warts which are white, and give it a sparkling appearance.

other half. There is a cave made of a few flat rocks, and here the animals spend all their time during these winter months.

Fat-tailed geckos used to be very costly. They sold for more than fifty dollars each. Now you can buy them for much less in large pet stores. These geckos belong to one of the species that will sometimes jump out of its skin, so be careful.

Pet stores import a little house gecko from Africa. This is about three or four inches long and is brown or tan, covered with little warts, some of which are snow white. They are nighttime animals, and remain quiet during the day. They like the same temperatures and cage furnishings as the fat-tailed geckos. They eat small insects and small meal-worms.

The United States does not have a very large gecko popula-

Banded Gecko. *Coleonyx variegatus.* These little animals live in the deserts of the West. They are nocturnal.

tion. There are a couple of species in the deserts of the West and Southwest, and a couple more in Florida. These are really not native to this country but were brought in on freight boats, as stowaways. They have bred enough in Florida to become established there.

Our prettiest specimen is the banded gecko of the southwestern deserts. These little animals are pinkish cream with chestnut spots on the skin. They like it hot and dry, and drink dewdrops. They also like to soak in a water dish, even though they come from desert lands. They eat insects, beetles, and grubs. These geckos can also jump out of their skins. The female lays one or two small white eggs under rocks or buried in loose ground.

CHAPTER 13

The Best Kinds of Skinks
to Keep as Pets

Any book on reptiles should mention skinks. They are an important group of animals, even though they do not make the very best pets. There are several reasons for this. Skinks are largely nocturnal, so you do not see them much in the daytime. They are generally nervous, frighten easily and cannot be handled very well. Also, skinks drop their tails quicker than almost any other reptile, so you are apt to end up with a stubby little animal the first time you try to play with it. These reptiles are secretive and hide most of the time under leaves, rotten logs, rocks, or trash on the ground. Some skinks are very brightly colored and are very beautiful.

Another aspect of skinks that makes them not very good pets is that they are very fast. Then, too, their scales are usually very smooth and shiny and their bodies are slender and slip out of your grasp very easily.

Once in a while you will find a specimen that is either braver than its brothers or for some reason is not so timid. This animal will allow itself to be picked up and handled a little. Do not relax your attention, however, or you will suddenly find yourself with empty hands except, maybe, for a squirming tail.

Five-lined Skink. *Eumeces fasciatus*. They are perfectly harmless and very beautiful animals.

Little Brown Skink. *Lygosoma laterale*. These animals are quite common in much of the United States. They are not easy to catch, though!

We have many species of skinks in this country. Probably the most colorful one is the common five-lined skink. Some of these have bright blue tails with pretty stripes on them. Some people fear these animals and claim that they are deadly poisonous. They may call them scorpions. True scorpions are called vinegarroons.

Another skink we have in the United States is the little brown skink. This is much smaller than the five-lined skink. It is light brown with tiny darker markings on the back. It is lighter on the belly. The same requirements and the same temperatures as for the five-lined skinks are good for these.

A curious member of the skink family is the cylindrical skink. At a quick first glance it might be mistaken for a small snake. When you look at it closely, though, you will see four tiny legs. These are so small and weak that you

Cylindrical Skink. *Chalcides chalcides*. The legs are so tiny on this animal that, for all practical purposes, they are useless.

wonder how the animal can use them to walk. Actually, it does not depend entirely upon the legs, but wriggles along much like a snake. I suppose that many hundreds of thousands of years from now the cylindrical skink will lose its legs altogether and look like the "glass snakes." Whenever an animal has some part of its body that it does not use very much, evolution slowly does away with that part and a new type of animal evolves.

Cylindrical skinks need the same food and conditions as the other skinks mentioned here. Cylindrical skinks are tamer than most other species. You can hold them in your hand without their being afraid. Now and then they will even take an insect from your fingers.

In recent years wholesale pet dealers have been importing many different animals from the Far East. One reason for this is that we have had wars all over that part of the world and we have had thousands and thousands of men over there. Some of these men are interested in nature and, in their spare time, collect animals to send back to our country. Also, professional hunters go where they can to find strange creatures. Pakistan and Malaysia are two places from which we have been receiving much material. From Pakistan we have been getting some very beautiful skinks. They call them golden-tailed skinks because they have bright golden-yellow tails. The backs are silver-gray and orange, and they are very pretty animals. Golden-tailed skinks are about six inches long. They eat meal-worms and other insects, and drink water out of a dish. They need a temperature a little higher than our skinks do. This is because they come from a warmer country. At night the temperature should not go below 55 degrees.

There are a great number of species of skinks in the world. Because they are so nervous, they should not be kept in

Golden-tailed Skink from Pakistan. I have been unable to identify this skink, but it is a very beautiful animal. The scales are very smooth and lie flat on the body.

cages. Some of them are very tiny little creatures. Others, like a couple from Australia, get to be 2 feet long—veritable giants of the skink family!

Skinks, like most other lizards, eat insects, grubs, worms, and insect larvae. In captivity they will eat meal-worms, crickets, grasshoppers, and beetles. They drink water out of a water dish, so that is not a problem. They like it fairly cool and moist, but not wet. A good cage setup for them is a few inches of clean soil mixed with a little sand. A layer of clean dead leaves on top of the dirt, a small log or two, and a piece of bark on top of the leaves will provide places for the animal to hide in. The temperature in the daytime should be around 70 degrees and can drop to as low as 50 or 55 at night.

CHAPTER 14

Breeding Reptiles

Breeding reptiles in captivity is a real challenge. First of all, animals do not readily breed unless the conditions under which they are being kept are close to those they are used to in their natural habitat. This makes it all the more important that you do as much as you can to see that you make them comfortable and keep them contented.

Sometimes you may get a reptile—a snake, for instance, or a lizard—and a short time after you bring it home and put it into its cage, it will lay some eggs or have some live young. This is not really breeding the reptile. It merely means that the animal mated in the wild before it was caught. It bore its young regardless of the fact that it was confined in strange conditions. The mating urge is very strong. It is the way the species is kept alive.

In nature, purely by instinct, the female finds the spot to lay her eggs that is most nearly perfect for them. She is not always successful, and sometimes the eggs die before hatching, and there are no young from that pair that year.

Reptile eggs are not quite like the eggs you have each morning for breakfast. The shells of reptile eggs are soft and flexible. They are also *porous*. This means that you can very easily drown a reptile egg by making it too wet. The water will seep right through the porous shell of the egg and dilute the insides until the embryo drowns. It also means that you can kill a reptile egg by allowing it to dry out, because the moisture inside the egg can evaporate through the porous shell and the embryo dies from lack of moisture.

From all this, you can see that keeping a reptile egg in the right state until it hatches is a touchy thing. In nature the female reptile finds places that are damp but not wet, places where the egg is protected from the wind so that it will not dry out. The place must be protected from the sun so that it will not bake, but must be warm enough for the embryo to develop inside the shell. She finds places where predators will not be liable to come across the eggs and eat them before they have hatched, but are open enough to allow the tiny helpless young reptiles to find their way to freedom after they come out of the shell.

All this is done by an instinct that was developed over many millions of years. If you had the same instincts, breeding reptiles would be easy. Since you do not have them, you must use the next best thing. The next best thing to instinct, in this case, is reason. You must reason out what would be the best way to take care of the eggs your pets may lay for you.

The first thing you should do is to remove the eggs from the cage where your pets are kept. In the wild, a reptile lays her eggs, then goes off about her business, never seeing the eggs again unless by accident. If she did come across the eggs, there is a good chance that she would eat them. In a cage, there is hardly any chance that she *won't* eat them.

When you start out to breed reptiles, you should plan the whole thing from the beginning. You do not just catch or buy two animals and decide to let them have young. You prepare for it. First of all, find out everything you possibly can about that particular species of reptile. A call to the keeper of reptiles in your local zoo may pay dividends. If he cannot help you right away, he usually has an excellent list of books with the information in them. Sometimes the curator of reptiles in a large natural history museum will know about the kinds of reptiles you want to breed.

I don't know of a single curator or zoo keeper who will not take the time and trouble to answer any questions from a boy or girl who is honestly and sincerely interested in learning something about a species of animal. If you approach these people and let them know that you want to know certain things because you are really interested in gaining additional knowledge, they should be most happy and willing to help you. A letter or a phone call will do or pay a visit to their laboratories if that is possible.

If you offer to let them know the results of your experiments, to tell them exactly what you did try to get good results, and the way your efforts turned out, you will show them that you mean business. Remember that even a beginner can discover something that was not known before about the management of a certain reptile, and when you do discover something, the knowledge should be spread immediately among those people who spend their lives in research in this area. You may not even know that you found something new. The scientist would know, however, and he would be very grateful to find out from you.

All this means that you should go about your attempts in breeding with a regular plan in mind. You should keep a notebook. Write down in it when, where, and how you got your reptiles. Write down all the things you did to set them up in their cage, *how* you fed them and *what* you fed them. Note how much they ate, and whether they seemed

Green Lacertas mating. *Lacerta viridis.* When he has a good hold on the female, the male turns his body upside down to bring their cloacas into contact.

Green Lacertas mating. The male keeps a hold on the female, with his mouth, and also holds her head close to him with his front leg. He does not bite her so hard that it hurts her.

to like it and eat it eagerly, or just ate it to keep alive. Write down the date and the time of the day that they mated, and—this is very important—describe the mating procedure as carefully as you can. What the male did and how he did it. What the female did and how she did it. How long they mated. Note the conditions of temperature and climate at the time—was it hot, dry, humid, cold, daytime, nighttime? All these little things are bits of knowledge which, put together, describe the life history of that particular kind of animal.

If you have a pair of reptiles that you want to breed, and you are able to keep them under conditions that will induce them to mate, you should, after they have mated, think about setting up a brooder or incubator in which to keep the eggs. A flat rectangular dish is ideal for this purpose. There are many sizes of ovenproof glass dishes for cooking and baking that will serve. Select one that is not too large (or too small, either), and in the bottom lay a folded paper towel that was wet and wrung out as dry as possible. If there is standing water in the towel, your eggs will drown.

When the eggs are laid, put them on this damp towel, cover them with another paper towel, also wet and wrung out dry, and then cover the whole dish with a sheet of glass. Put the brooder in a dark place where it is just slightly warm—neither too hot, nor too cool. Reptile eggs take a long time to hatch. Every few days you should look at them to see that the towels are still very slightly damp, and that the air inside the brooder is humid.

The eggs should hatch after four to twelve weeks. The young reptiles are very active at birth, and can scamper in all directions when you open the brooder. Do *not* put the young ones back in the cage with their parents. They will last just long enough to be swallowed by either the male or the female, whichever catches them first!

Eggs of the "Glass Snake." As soon as you are sure that the animal is finished laying her eggs, you should remove them to an incubator. If you leave them with the mother, the chance is good that she will eat them!

Reptiles that have their young alive are somewhat easier to provide for. Naturally, a brooder does not have to be maintained. The young must be removed from the cage as fast as they are born, however, to keep them from being eaten. If the mating was observed, then you should, about four or five weeks later, put the female in a separate cage, alone, to have her young. This will give some of the tiny ones a chance. The male often will stay near the female when she is giving birth, eating the young as fast as they are produced. This may seem horrible to you or me, but it is perfectly natural for this animal. Anything small enough and alive is food to reptiles. They have practically no maternal instinct. (Maternal instinct is high in some mammals and highest in the human race.)

Jackson's Chameleon. Minutes after they are born, the tiny animals are wandering all over the bush looking for food.

Since none of this maternal instinct is present in reptiles, the mother and father reptile do not even know that the young ones they are gobbling up so fast are their own. They are merely food for them. If you know this and understand the reason for it, then you will see that there is nothing at all wrong or horrible about a reptile eating its own young. You merely have to think for them. You have to protect the little ones against their enemies—in this case, bigger reptiles.

Food is the most important single factor in rearing young reptiles. The little ones need food almost as soon as they are hatched or born. They need it small enough for them to swallow. Mostly, they need live food, because they eat very little food in nature that is not alive.

Long before your eggs hatch or the female gives birth to her young, you should have your food supply ready— a meal-worm farm with plenty of tiny worms for lizards and snakes; fruit-fly farms for anoles, chameleons, and almost any other kind of lizard. These will supply the needed small food for the young.

If, after the young animals start to grow, some become much larger than the others, the larger ones should be separated from the smaller ones because they, too, will eat the smaller ones if there is enough difference in size.

CHAPTER 15

Releasing Reptiles That Have Been Tamed

As a fitting end to a book on keeping reptiles, here are a few words on what to do with them after you no longer can or want to keep them.

As with most animals, reptiles, mammals, or birds, once the specimen has been kept long enough in captivity, there is a better than even chance that it will be unable to survive if released. This may be truer of mammals and birds than it is of reptiles, but still reptiles lose, to a degree, the ability to survive once they have been tamed.

Of course, the greatest danger is that, having been tamed, the animal is no longer so afraid of man. After release, it may wander right up to a house or place where people live and be promptly killed.

The next thing to consider is that the creature will be unable to get food. Having become used to finding its food right under its nose, so to speak, it can no longer trace its prey, run it down, and capture it.

All these things should be taken into consideration when you want to release a reptile that you have had for some time. Another important item to remember is the location from which the animal originally came. If it was native to this country, and came from a section where the climate is much the same as yours, there can be no great danger in letting it go as far as food or temperature is concerned. The fact that it may be the only specimen of its species in your area is not good, though.

Whenever possible, it is much kinder to ship the creature back where it came from, either to the person from whom you obtained it in the beginning, or to an interested person who would receive it and liberate it for you. You might write to a school science teacher, for instance, asking him if he would allow you to send him a specimen for him to release when it arrived.

If the animal came from a tropical country or the desert and if you live in a Temperate Zone or in the East or Far West, certainly you should not just dump it out and expect it to live. In this case, you should find someone else who might like to have it as a pet and who would care for it as you did.

Very often a museum will take all kinds of specimens to study. If a museum is doing a study of any animal, the researchers will need many specimens, so the chances of being able to get rid of your surplus is much better at a museum than a zoo. Always call or write first. Do not just take the animal to the museum until you find out whether it will be accepted. In your call or letter, make sure that the person in charge understands that you are giving it, not trying to sell an animal that might not be needed.

You see, it is not so simple as taking a reptile outside and sending it on its way. Many factors should be taken into consideration before releasing animals. Think of some of these things even before you get your pet.

Appendix: Scientific Names

POPULAR NAME	SCIENTIFIC NAME
Hybrid pine snake	*Pituophis melanoleucus*
Common king snake	*Lampropeltis g. getulus*
Eastern king snake	*Lampropeltis g. getulus*
Southern king snake	*Lampropeltis g. holbrooki*
Milk snake	*Lampropeltis t. triangulum*
Corn snake	*Elaphe g. guttata*
Green rat snake	*Elaphe obsoleta quadrivittata*
Black snake	*Elaphe o. obsoleta*
Fox snake	*Elaphe vulpina*
Boa constrictor	*C. constrictor*
Reticulated python	*Python reticulatus*
Rainbow boa	*Epicrates cenchris*
Indigo snake	*Drymarchon corais couperi*
California red-sided garter snake	*Thamnophis sirtalis parietalis*
Marcy's garter snake	*Thamnophis marcianus*
Ribbon snake	*Thamnophis sauritus proximus*
Hog-nosed snake	*Heterodon platyrhinos*
DeKay's snake	*Storeria dekayi*
Sonora snake (ground snake)	*Sonora episcopa*
Egg-eating snake	*Dasypeltis scabra*
Tentacled water snake	*Erpetron tentaculatum*
Water snake	*Natrix taxispilota*
Red-bellied snake	*Farancia abacura*
Ring-necked snake	*Diadophis p. punctatus*
Rubber boa	*Charina bottae*
Red-eared turtle	*Pseudemys scripta elegans*

Map turtle	*Graptemys geographica*
Snapping turtle	*Chelydra serpentina*
Saw-backed turtle	*Graptemys nigrinoda*
Eastern painted turtle	*Chrysemys picta picta*
Western painted turtle	*Chrysemys picta belli*
Southern painted turtle	*Chrysemys picta dorsalis*
Siamese pond turtle	*Malayemys subtrijuga*
Spotted turtle	*Clemmys guttata*
Musk turtle	*Sternothaerus odoratus*
Yellow mud turtle	*Kinosternon f. flavescens*
Wood turtle	*Clemmys insculpta*
Common box turtle	*Terrapene c. carolina*
Blanding's box turtle	*Emydoidea blandingi*
Three-toed box turtle	*Terrapene c. triunguis*
Ornate box turtle	*Terrapene ornata ornata*
American "chameleon"	*Anolis carolinensis*
Fence lizard	*Sceloporus undulatus*
European wall lizard	*Lacerta muralis albanica*
Basilisk	*Basiliscus americanus*
Alligator lizard	*Gerrhonotus multicarinatus*
"Horned toad"	*Phrynosoma coronatum*
Desert spiny lizard	*Sceloporus magister*
Collared lizard	*Crotaphytus c. collaris*
"Glass snake"	*Ophisauris attenuatus*
Cayman	*Caiman sclerops*
Armadillo lizard	*Cordylus cataphractus*
Green lacerta	*Lacerta viridis*
Iguana	*Iguana iguana*
African chameleon	*Chamaeleo jacksoni*
Tokay gecko	*Gekko gecko*
Pakistani striped gecko	*Unidentified*
Leopard gecko	*Eublephorus macularis*
African house gecko	*Hemidactylus species*
Banded gecko	*Coleonyx variegatus*
Five-lined skink	*Eumeces fasciatus*
Little brown skink	*Lygosoma laterale*
Cylindrical skink	*Chalcides chalcides*
Golden-tailed skink	*Unidentified*

Index

About the Author

PAUL VILLIARD, the author of REPTILES AS PETS, was born in Spokane, Washington, and now lives in Saugerties, New York. Although he started out as a mechanical engineer, he soon found that his real talent lay in writing about and photographing nature.

He has traveled for many years in the Pacific islands, South America, and the entire United States. From these years of traveling, observing, and photographing came much of the material for this book. But along the way he got interested in subjects other than nature, and is the author of candy and cookie cookbooks, a plumbing and heating guide, and a manual of veneering.

In production at this time, to be released this year, are a book on the rearing of exotic moths, a book of ceramics, another on jewelry-making, and an autobiographic novel telling the story of the author's days as a young boy. A book on nature photography for young people is also in work, to be published by Doubleday in 1969.

His beautiful photography and fine writing have appeared in *Natural History, Audubon* magazine, *Popular Home Craft, Home Crafts and Hobbies, Reader's Digest,* and *Nature and Science* magazine, among others.